WOMEN & SUCCESS

WOMEN & SUCCESS
POLLYANNA LENKIC

BAKER STREET PRESS

© Pollyanna Lenkic 2015

First Published in 2015 by Baker Street Press | Melbourne
Reprinted in 2015

ISBN 978-0-9943214-0-4

National Library of Australia Cataloguing-in-Publication entry:

Creator: Lenkic, Pollyanna, author.
Title: Women & success / Pollyanna Lenkic.
ISBN: 9780994321404 (paperback)
Notes: Includes bibliographical references.
Subjects: Self-actualization (Psychology) in women. Women--Life skills guides. Success.
Dewey Number: 158.1082

Edited by Joanna Yardley
Cover design by Flight Creative

All rights reserved. No part of this publication may be reproduced by any means without the prior written consent of the publisher.

While much of this book is supported by personal experiences and to the best of my memory, I have also included case studies of remarkable women who have shared their stories. In most cases, names and personal information have been changed to preserve anonymity. I would like to thank these women for their generous contribution and congratulate them on their successes. Pollyanna Lenkic.

Pollyanna Lenkic is brilliant at separating the humanistic from the gender issues plaguing business today. Her take on women in business is practical and honest and fills me with hope for its ability to rewire perceptions and redefine the challenge for increasing 'women in leadership'. Her approach on what it means to be an adult is such a clarion call for the kinds of behaviours that set, in my opinion, businesses and cultures on the right path.

Matt Church, founder of *Thought Leaders Global*, author of *Amplifiers* and *Adrenaline Junkies and Serotonin Seekers*, co-author of *Sell Your Thoughts* and 2014 Australian speaker of the year

*

Pollyanna is an amazing Thought Leader who is developing ground-breaking thinking into how women sabotage themselves by collapsing human issues with gender issues, and what it takes to be successful in business and life in the 21st century. But this book will do much more than give you insight into what it takes to be successful, it will actually guide you through a self-paced process to determine what success actually means for you, and how to get out of the way so that you live life on your terms.

Peter Cook, Dean of *Thought Leaders Business School* and co-author of *Sell Your Thoughts*

*

Pollyanna Lenkic is one of the most sophisticated coaches I know. In this book, she's woven together the big picture from her *Women & Success* survey, personal stories from women like you, and her own coaching expertise to provide a manual that will provide both insight and the tools for action.

Michael Bungay Stanier, author of *Do More Great Work* and senior partner at *Box of Crayons*

I want to acknowledge your investment in you; the best investment you can make. It's time to accept graciously your success.

Pollyanna

CONTENTS

- CONTENTS VIII
- PREFACE XI
- ACKNOWLEDGEMENTS XII
- INTRODUCTION 17
- **CH.1 AN EXPLORATION OF SUCCESS** 23
  - HOW IT ALL BEGAN 23
  - ACTION WITHOUT VISION 24
  - JOURNEY TO INSIGHT AND SELF-DISCOVERY 26
  - JOURNEY TO ACCOUNTABILITY 29
- **CH.2 WOMEN, WORK & SUCCESS** 33
  - PART ONE 33
- **CH.3 WOMEN, WORK & SUCCESS** 41
  - PART TWO 41
- **CH.4 NEEDS** 49
  - MASLOW'S ORIGINAL 5 HIERARCHY OF NEEDS 60
- **CH.5 BELIEFS** 63
- **CH.6 LIMITING BELIEFS** 67
- **CH.7 SELF-SABOTAGE:**
- **THE SUCCESS TERMINATOR** 75
  - THE SABOTEUR'S CONVENTION 79
  - THE LOYAL SOLDIER 79
  - IT'S OUR JOB TO MANAGE OUR SELF-SABOTAGE 81

THE SABOTEUR'S CYCLE	83
THE CHAMPION	84
THE CHAMPION'S CYCLE	85

CH.8 MISERY OR JOY:

HOW DO YOU WANT TO LIVE	93
CONSCIOUSLY CHOOSING JOY	95

CH.9 PERFECTION:

LIFE'S GREATEST CON	113
CH.10 TAKE A STAND FOR YOU	121
CH.11 BE YOUR BEST SELF	127
BE THE BEST VERSION OF YOU	127
SURVEY OF CHARACTER	131
CH.12 CHANGE THE SENTENCE	135
CH.13 SUCCESS AND HOW YOU FEEL	143
CH.14 MAKE SPACE FOR CELEBRATION	147

CH.15 JUGGLING:

THE ADDICTION THAT LEADS TO EXHAUSTION	159
DECISIONS	164

CH.16 VALUES:

UNDERSTANDING WHAT DRIVES THE CORE OF YOU	169
CH.17 COMMUNICATION, POSITIONING AND SUCCESS	183
ONLY USE 'I' WHEN YOU OWN IT	193
AFTERWORD	**203**

GLOSSARY 205

SUPPORT GROUPS LIST 205

CONTRIBUTORS AND SPECIAL MENTIONS 206

MORE ABOUT THE AUTHOR 214

WOMEN TALK ABOUT SUCCESS 215

PREFACE

As a woman, making this personal investment will generate a positive effect on you, your children, your nieces and nephews, and other children who are important to you.

You can always find reasons to focus outside of yourself and buy into the excuses for doing so. Investing in *you* takes courage, love and commitment; I applaud you for embarking upon this journey—your journey.

This is where you will uncover more about *you* and what is important to *you*. Within this book, you will be given the tools to help you achieve more of what *you* want—*that's a worthy investment to make for the sake of you.*

Here are three suggestions on how to use this book:

1. Read and enjoy the conversations and stories shared by the women who have contributed to the important messages surrounding women and success.

2. Set aside time each week to read, to keep a journal of ideas and inspirations that come to mind, and to complete the exercises.

3. Invite your friends to form a *success circle*. Commit to reading the book together; gather weekly to talk about the impact the book is creating in your lives. Explore common themes: where you get stuck; what excites you. Keep each other accountable for making the changes that you want to make—support each other.

ACKNOWLEDGEMENTS

I am incredibly grateful to all the people who have helped me on my journey so far; they are numerous. Some have been in my life for many years, others are more recent, but without you this work and my passion in supporting women to live fulfilled lives would never have eventuated. You held me accountable and demanded that I step up, thank you.

From the first moment I questioned how women viewed success, I have been inspired. I am consumed with drive and passion. This is the work I am meant to be doing; the work that I love doing and for this, I am truly grateful. The greatest excitement of all is that I can ignite conversation and exploration surrounding women and success so that it can continue to grow. I am committed to raising the conversation to include men as well as women, so that together we can create the life and success we desire—not only appreciate it but to acknowledge this within ourselves.

Thank you to all the women who have shared their journey with me and who graciously allowed me to share their stories via the case studies in this book.

At 24 years of age, I was presented an opportunity to partner in building an IT recruitment business in London, to get that business to a place where my business partner would be able to give up his day job and work on the business full-time thus making real a dream he had held for a long time. I am grateful for that opportunity and the support I had from both my business partner, in that adventure, and the many others who supported me.

I also acknowledge that I made the most of that opportunity. I worked incredibly hard and slew quite a few negative thoughts and beliefs in the process (or at least silenced them enough to get on with it!). It resulted in creating revenue that made it possible to take the business from a small part-time hobby to an £11 million turnover company employing 18 full-time team members and 100+ consultants on various client sites throughout the UK. It was an amazing experience of which to be a part. It helped shape the direction of my future through success and self-doubt and eventually leading to understanding and growth. I love and am grateful for the rich experiences this opportunity offered.

Over 15 years ago, I attended the Coaches Training Institute's (CTI) course in London and then went on to complete their certification program and their Leadership program in the USA. This training and development was truly life changing and set me up with the skills and hunger to do the work that I was meant to do in the world.

Having honed this skill over many years, I was fortunate to discover Thought Leaders Business School, which has given me the approach, the methodology and the accountability to launch my work with more depth, structure and value to the clients I serve.

My heartfelt thanks go to the founders of Thought Leaders, Matt Church and Peter Cook for the mentoring, the structure and the no-excuses accountability that their Thought Leaders Business School provides. Thought Leaders is a community of which I am privileged and proud to be a part. Without them this book would not have been written; it would have stayed in the, *I'd love to do that one day* category.

To my dear friend and colleague Sandi Bookatz. The years we spent working together added depth, learning and richness to my life and the work I do. Thank you.

To Amanda Gome, thanks for pushing me into writing for SmartCompany many years ago. This discipline and practice made this book possible.

To my wonderful mentor Corrinne Armour whose steady support has kept me moving forward with this project and others.

A special thank you and mention to my editor Joanna Yardley from The Editing House. THANK YOU. Working with you from the onset has made a huge difference to the quality, structure and completion of this project. Thank you for all your brainstorming and for turning my words into a format that flows, and all done while maintaining my voice and authenticity in the message I want to share.

To my daughters Ella Rose and Niamh Maisie who inspire me to be the best person I can be and who have brought an abundance of joy and love into my world.

To my husband Sean, without you I couldn't do what I do. Your partnership and love ground me and keep me solid. Thank you for all the weekends you took the girls out to play so I could write, and for your continuing support of me and the work that drives me.

For Ella Rose and Niamh Maisie

There came a time when the risk to remain tight in the bud was more painful than the risk it took to blossom.

Anaïs Nin

INTRODUCTION

My journey is your journey—a shared journey uniting millions of women globally. We may live in different parts of the world and come from different cultures and beliefs; however, as women, we are connected by our journey and experiences. We have common themes that derail us, unite us and move us forward in life.

We are all unique and individual and have our own paths to lead. Our challenges are also unique—except, for when they are not.

There are themes, patterns and blocks that have immerged, which show a commonality about how women perceive and experience success, how we run toward success, and how we run away from success.

We have complex strategies for sabotaging our success, often with an inability to acknowledge and celebrate the success we do achieve. We brush it off as an accident: *you just got lucky*, or *you were in the right place at the right time*. This type of thinking dominates and negates the hard work and investment that went before.

Your success isn't an accident. It's a culmination of your effort, your investment and your talent ...

... And now it's time to identify it, own it and savour it.

Your lack of success and fulfilment is *not* about your abilities, your talents or lack thereof, or what you may or may not believe about worth and entitlement. Nor is it about whether or not you feel you deserve success.

It *is*, however, about *not* taking the time to invest in your own life. Discover what's important to you; set boundaries and move ferociously toward the life you want to live. To do this it's important to understand the core of you: What makes you who you are? How does this impact those around you, and the contribution you make to your communities and the world? By understanding the core of you, you are building *your* successful life as defined by *you*.

Success is intensely personal and yet so public. We measure ourselves and others by *factors* such as rank, status, clothes, wealth etc. and we have predetermined that these *factors* define our feelings surrounding our success and the success of others.

How often have you taken the time really to look at what success means to you?

There are many fabulous books which explore success. *Amazon* lists 223,002 such books. While these books will tell you how to develop a *success* mindset and explain the psychology of success, *Women & Success* is about helping you to identify your own success.

Women & Success will encourage you to recognise how *you* feel about success; how *you* define success; and what success means to *you*. *Women & Success* is dedicated to women. It heralds from research I conducted (*Women, Work & Success*, 2006) on how women perceive and define themselves through the lens of success. It is based on years of personal and professional experiences while working with thousands of women, both in Australia and in the UK, and *my* personal journey of discovery—I want this book to be *your* personal journey of discovery and more.

Insight and discovery are essential before any journey begins and before any plan is implemented. However, for your journey to be truly effective, it must be accompanied by action.

Therefore, begin your journey by:

— asking yourself what success means to you

— developing a solid foundation on which to build a successful life, which has been defined by you and is truly meaningful to you

— examining and questioning your current beliefs about what success means to you

— challenging your thinking and beliefs. Is your current formula working? Is it sustainable? Is this the formula from which you want to continue to build your life?

— creating an action plan and locking in accountabilities.

Throughout this book you will share in the stories of other women; you will laugh with them; you will shed a tear with them; and you will spend time reflecting on what their stories mean to you.

I have designed various exercises that are beneficial in getting the maximum value from this book. Revisit the exercises that are most helpful—this will help you to measure where you are at, to see what has remained constant and what has shifted. You can then:

— uncover the themes that emerge

— gain deeper insight about you and your journey

— create a pattern for stronger conversations with your family, friends and work colleagues about success and your experiences

- grow by listening to the experiences of others
- understand where you are aligned and where you are not
- add richness to the diversity of your beliefs and mindset
- create a plan that aligns to *your* personal meaning of success rather than chasing someone else's success blueprint.

Vision without action is a daydream. Action without vision is a nightmare.

Japanese proverb

Courage is not the absence of fear, but rather the judgement that something else is more important than fear.

James Neil Hollingworth

CH.1 AN EXPLORATION OF SUCCESS

HOW IT ALL BEGAN

It's November 2000. The sun is setting and I'm sitting on a beach in Kenya having just completed my 8th skydive for the day. I am surrounded by great people and I have nothing to do but repack my rig for another day of jumping.

Externally it's idyllic, relaxed and peaceful. Internally, a very different scene is playing. A deep underlying tension is running through me; it's been there so long, it's become a part of me—accepted as a normal way of being.

"Miss Pollyanna, Miss Pollyanna." I look up and see one of the hotel staff holding a banner with my name of it. "Fax for Miss Pollyanna."

I tense. A huge wave of anxiety takes hold. I am gripped with fear, hope and anticipation: would this fax bring more problems or finally release me?

I take the folded piece of paper and hold it for a while. I take a breath and open it. It is from my lawyer in London and she had written two words, *you're free*. I double over and cry all the tears that I had been holding inside for the past two years.

Released from the pressure valve that was selling my share of The Company[1]—of which, I had the privilege of building—a new anxiety gripped me with overwhelming intensity. What would I do now? Was I capable of doing something else? How would I introduce myself now that I'm no longer a director?

---

[1] The Company was SQ Computer Personnel

I immediately reprimanded myself for having those thoughts. *It's ridiculous*, I told myself. You have your whole future ahead of you; you have choices. Others had always told me how lucky I was: why wasn't I feeling lucky at that moment?

When we are faced with an open book of choices it can be overwhelming.

In the following 18 months, my world continued to change at a rapid pace. I unravelled the person I was—transforming into the person I was meant to be.

My journey had just begun …

ACTION WITHOUT VISION

I landed in London in 1986. I was 21. I didn't know anyone. I had £40 in my pocket.

I was determined not to call my parents for help. £40 was enough to pay for a few nights' accommodation at a hotel in Paddington that catered for backpackers, but I would have to find work quickly.

Within 24 hours, I had picked up a job as a chambermaid, working alongside the other broke backpackers—that took care of accommodation and breakfast.

It was a fun time; I formed great friendships and life felt like one big adventure (much like the previous nine months travelling Europe).

Somehow, from there I built an amazing life in London. I met fabulous people and felt very much at home (for 17 years) in one of the world's greatest cities. I had many adventures and a few misadventures.

In 1990, I was offered the opportunity to work on building a business with my partner at the time. It was an IT recruitment company: a profession I knew nothing about. I remember thinking, *I'll give it six months, and if it doesn't work, I'll find something else.* I set up a room in our home and begun the task of working out what a recruitment consultant did.

In the early days, I would sit and stare at my newly created, tidy office and think, *what do I do now?* It was daunting: I was 24 and I didn't know what I was doing or what to do next.

But I found my rhythm. I dived headfirst into learning everything I could about the industry. I leaned on those around me—who had expertise—and with support from my partner, began to build momentum. The plan was to build the business to a point where it would provide an income for both of us, giving my partner the freedom to leave contracting and join me. I achieved my goal and it was one of my proudest moments.

I worked hard over the next ten years building a client base and business. My life was centred on growing and learning The Company. Through the years of investment my confidence increased. Most of my social connections came from the work I did—fabulous people, many of whom I am still connected to today.

My work became my identity, how I defined myself. I poured everything I had into my work. At the time it didn't feel like an issue. I felt fortunate because I loved the job I preformed every day—going to the office was a joy.

The problem was that my work became the main focus for who I was. My sense of self and self-worth was tied to what I did, not who I was.

The focus was on what I was doing as opposed to who I was being. I was so entrenched in my work and my role that it became impossible to imagine myself doing anything else. *This is a common state many people find themselves in when their work becomes the sole focus of who they are.* The single focus and attachment of work can often crowd out other aspects of life, which may not be as fulfilling. This results in avoiding the less satisfying aspects of our life and relationships.

Separating myself from this identity was the beginning of my self-discovery journey. It was the birth of a new awareness and launched me into a new life and career, which I now feel privileged to live.

JOURNEY TO INSIGHT AND SELF-DISCOVERY

My partner and I worked hard to build the business. We expanded from a sole-employee entity to staff of 18, with a contract workforce of over 100 consultants and an annual turnover in excess of £11m.

In 2000, I sold my 50% shareholding.

Things had changed. I knew with every fibre of my being that The Company would not survive if my partner and I continued to work together: one of us would have to move on. We had a dedicated team who relied upon the business; they had dedicated their energy and efforts to help build The Company; they had lives and mortgages to pay. The decision to move on wasn't just about what was best for me.

At the time, I was terrified—it was one of the bravest and most frightening decisions I had ever made. It was a decision based on values. I knew deep down that staying would destroy me. In order to move on I needed to leave the business that had been my life for 10 years. The fear of staying felt immense. It was like climbing a mountain without being able to see the summit and not knowing how high it was. However, I realised that the fear of staying, and what that meant, was far greater than the fear of embarking on such a significant change and having to deal with unravelling both personal and business issues, and financial settlements.

At first it wasn't an easy transition. My personal life was also unravelling, and everything was changing. My 10-year relationship with my business partner/husband was at an end. My career had ended, and I was trying to work out the next step. The anchors that hold people in place when a break up happens—work and home—were no longer solid places for me. I felt adrift.

The turning point came one evening while sitting at my kitchen table with my beautiful friend Amanda Simoes. I had a glass of wine in my hand and was crying about the uncertainty of my future. Amanda had also just come out of a long-term relationship and was experiencing the same loss. So I invited Amanda to share my home – a decision that redirected me on a healthier route. I proposed that we support each other: I would provide her with a home and she would provide me with personal training (part of my healthier route).

However, Amanda provided so much more. I removed all the wine from the house—it didn't feel right to have alcohol in the house with a recovered alcoholic. This decision kept me healthy and focused. It wasn't an easy journey … valuable ones rarely are.

Amanda shared her journey with me and I decided to deal with my issues with a clear head. I would *face* my life—and its overwhelming uncertainties—rather than hiding from and numbing the experience.

It's interesting how scenes can play out differently—internally and externally. I sold my shareholding six months before the IT downturn. Others thought I was savvy: How did I know? What prompted the timing? Of course it had nothing to do with the market or timing. The decision was thrust upon me and I was reluctantly going along for the ride.

I looked like I had it all: I drove a Porsche, wore designer clothes, and skydived most weekends in glamourous places around the world. I was the picture of a *success story*. Yet, as you know now, I felt anything but a success. I wondered how there could be such disconnect between how you are seen and how you are feeling? I felt guilty for feeling that way when I had achieved so much and was set financially.

JOURNEY TO ACCOUNTABILITY

My friendship with Amanda had set me on a healthier path, both physically and mentally. I was on a path of self-discovery and healing. Skydiving was also a great saviour: to be safe around others in the sky, you need a clear head. There is a fabulous unrestricted spirit in the skydiving community and I was fortunate to have some solid anchors in my life, which I came to realise as the months and years rolled on.

I invested in a great counsellor who helped me deal with the past, take accountability for my past actions and transition to a new life. I enrolled in a coaching course with the Coaches Training Institute and invested in obtaining certification—a decision that would endure the journey of discovery and accountability and would shape my life and future career in a positive way. I was beginning to stretch myself and break free from the bonds of limiting beliefs about who I was and what the future would hold.

After my coach training I progressed to the Co-Active Leadership Program, which deepened my learning and development, and redefined what I thought was possible. I was beginning to realise what others before me already knew well: that to undergo a transformational journey, you must learn to lead a fulfilled life. You must grow and learn by looking at yourself and doing the work you need to do on yourself before you work with others.

Throughout all of this, a deep curiosity was growing. What was success? What did it mean to me? What did it mean to other women? How do we, as women, define ourselves through success?

I began having conversations with other women about what success meant to them? Did they feel successful?

In 2012, I moved back to Australia with my partner Sean. We live in Melbourne with our two beautiful daughters. Clearly the decision to swear off love and relationships (fortunately) didn't stick.

The most significant social change in the last three decades has been the large scale entry of women into the workforce. At the same time, the world of work itself has been changing and the goal posts for success have become obsolete.

Women, Work & Success Survey 2006

CH.2 WOMEN, WORK & SUCCESS

PART ONE

The burning curiosity about women and success continued to grow. I wanted to learn more about how women felt about success; about their relationship with success; and how this impacted their lives. To extend upon this conversation, I set up a survey.

In 2006, I designed and launched the research project into women, work and success. *Women, Work & Success* was a first of its kind report identifying the need for up-to-date information about how Australian women perceived success. It was conducted within Australia, and resulted from responses from a statistically representative sample of women across a broad range of industries working in professional and management positions.

In a talk to 250+ professional leaders, I shared my findings and the top 5 factors that contribute to success in women's lives and careers. It was an interactive session aimed at creating discussion and stimulating thoughts about what success meant at a personal level; how it translated professionally and how that aligned with the organisations in which women worked.

Here is it, unedited …

Thanks Sue, for the warm introduction.

It's a pleasure to be here in beautiful Melbourne presenting to you all.

I would like to express my gratitude to everyone who has supported me through my Women & Success research; the women who completed the survey and shared their valuable thoughts; our speakers who have made this a memorable event and the WIMBN[2] group who are totally committed to supporting women to be successful.

Speaking to everyone prior to this event, it is evident that there is a real desire to contribute, share and to add value.

As you will hear, contribution and community are important values for women, and honouring and sharing those values bring about the success of today's event. Can you imagine the possibilities if you too, were to honour those values?

I first became curious about what success means to women in November 2000. I had returned to London from a great-skydiving holiday in Kenya—I came close to not returning after knocking myself out at 15,000 feet (not a smart move) but that's a different story—and was celebrating the sale of The Company with some incredibly successful female friends.

As we were chatting and the girls were congratulating me on my achievements with The Company, I found myself saying things like, 'Oh well, I was in the right place at the right time. I was lucky, it wasn't really down to me'.

---

[2] Women in Mortgage Business Network: A former organisation in support of successful women.

Sound familiar?

Our attention moved to Amy. She was talking about all the things that had gone wrong on one of her projects—there was no mention on what had gone well, which was a lot.

Sara had just launched an offshore fund; it was a very successful project. She was on the news (our friend on the BBC ... WOW). She piped up with, 'God, I am so hacked off—not what she really said, just keeping it polite—for not doing ABC ...'. At that point, my mind screamed, what was going on?

Two things stood out for me:

1. No one seated at this table owned their accomplishments.

2. We were unclear about what success really meant to us, and how we defined ourselves through success.

All five women seated at that table we were 100% focusing on the 10% that didn't go well, and not acknowledging the 90% that did go well.

I got curious: What is this all about? Did all women think like this? Like all things that are meaningful, it took hold and evolved.

Looking back at that time, the most amusing thing for me is that I was heralded as a smart, savvy businesswoman for selling The Company six months prior to the IT crash. That was so far from the truth. People often asked me why I sold: did I foresee something in the market? I simply made a decision based upon my values.

What I valued at the time was the freedom to move on with my life, and I knew I couldn't do that if I stayed tied to the business in any way. I took a deep breath and moved away from everything that was familiar to me. I was terrified.

When I returned to Australia, four years ago, I began searching for information on what Australian women think: there wasn't much available. I'm delighted that now, there is.

Here are some of the highlights from my Women & Success survey (some things that stood out for me).

— 91.3% of the women surveyed feel successful.

— Women consider multiple vital factors in achieving success for themselves and the organisation for which they work.

— Success, for women, is not measured by the title 'manager' or by pay rises. What is important is seeking satisfaction, using skills and giving back to the community/society.

— Work/life balance and job satisfaction are rated higher than financial reward in terms of personal goals.

— Men and women perceive success differently: anyone surprised by this one? Let's look at that:

Yes, women do perceive success differently than men, and a survey conducted by Mainiero and Sullivan in 2005 revealed that women are path blazers in a nonlinear, relational approach to work and that males of generation X and Y are following in their wake.

I want you to take a moment to pause and think of the implications of this information ...

I stand for women feeling successful, and I want to raise global awareness of what success means to women, and I want to invite questions and discussion among both men and women. This is not a 'woman-only issue'. It's important for all of us to ask ourselves the question of what success means to us.

For the men in the audience: imagine how much more productive your professional and personal relationships with women will be when you take the time to understand what success means to women. As you come to understand the importance of this survey, you will realise that the findings are important to not just women, but to anyone who is in relationship with a woman—that's all of us.

Promoting success in a woman is very different to promoting success in a man. The traditional organisation is based on the conventional stimulus for male success.

Why develop an understanding of what success means to women?

Australia is facing a skills shortage due, in part, to an ageing population and lower workforce participation rate.

While women have entered the workforce in large numbers, their skills are under-utilised.

Employers can't afford to put their heads in the sand.

An example of creating a flexible work place environment appeared in the Herald Sun on the 22nd January 2006. The headline read:

New plan to lure medico mums back

To try to ease the crippling doctor shortage, the Queensland government is implanting [a] strategy to attract female doctors back into the system.

Government and leading organisations are becoming aware that they need to be able to attract and retain women in their workforce. In order to do this they need to develop an understanding of what women attribute to success.

Imagine the opportunities for greater success, when you expand the corporate environment in which women's success can continue to evolve. Employers need to compete for what women want as employees—what will make a successful environment for women will make a successful environment for men.

I invite you to explore what success means to you. Develop an understanding of your relationship with success, and be open to hearing what success means to others.

Ask yourself how you can apply that knowledge and understanding, and notice that as you invest time in learning what's important to you, the things you do in life connect to who you are.

For me, success is how I feel about who I am, my place in the world, the contribution I make, and the people in my life. It's about aligning the little things to the bigger picture of who I am being.

What does success mean to you?

Thank you

I want to do it because I want to do it. Women must try to do things as men have tried. When they fail, their failure must be but a challenge to others.

Amelia Earhart

CH.3 WOMEN, WORK & SUCCESS

PART TWO

I launched the *Women, Work & Success* survey because I wanted to know how Australian women define themselves through success. Of course, our understanding of success evolved over time.

The key findings of the *Women, Work & Success* survey have created a new opportunity for you and for your organisation. I invite you to take a fresh look at yourself and your relationship with success.

I am passionate about helping women achieve the success they desire. Promoting success in women is very different to promoting success in men. The traditional organisation is based on the conventional stimulus for male success.

Expanding the corporate environment in which success can continue to evolve for women will also have a positive impact on men who don't feel successful in traditional based organisations. This will transform the organisation as a whole.

KEY FINDINGS

- 91.3% of respondents feel successful.
- Women consider multiple factors to be vital in achieving success for themselves and the organisation.
- Women are overwhelmingly seeking rewarding work.
- Work/life balance and job satisfaction are rated more highly as goals than financial reward.
- Men and women perceive success differently.

- Women are seeking to make a difference – relational careers.
- 41% of women consider a flexible working environment to be one of the three key drivers of personal and organisational achievement.

SURVEY DEMOGRAPHICS

- 563 respondents.
- CEOs, managers, entrepreneurs and consultants …
- … from across a broad range of industries.
- First such survey in Australia across public and private sectors.

WHAT ORGANISATIONS NEED TO UNDERSTAND

- Biggest social change of the last three decades – large scale entry of women into the workforce.
- The world of work is changing.
- Organisations need flexibility to compete and achieve.
- Unlocking the potential of women's human capital to solve skills and labour shortages.
- The 'opt out' revolution.

WHEN ORGANISATIONS DON'T UNDERSTAND

- The failure of organisations to understand the different orientation women bring to success and work is the primary cause of women leaving organisations to begin their own business.

THE FACTORS FOR SUCCESS

— When asked to select the top three factors leading to a feeling of success in their lives, respondents identified good relationships (51.8%) and work/life balance (45.7%) well ahead of money (11.7%).

— When asked to nominate personal factors, relationships with partners and children, religion and spirituality, and giving back to the community featured prominently.

— In response to another question, respondents put family and friends (55.6%) and receiving love and support (43.3%) well ahead of such factors as academic achievement (6.9%), household management (22.4%) and being able to afford things (29.1%).

— Relational values and outcomes such as passion for one's occupation (82.3%) and getting along with others (38.2%) were similarly privileged over more mundane or instrumental inputs to work success.

— In summary, women use holistic measures for success rather than one dimensional factors such as financial security and academic or work related achievements.

WHAT CONTRIBUTES TO SUCCESS IN YOUR CAREER?

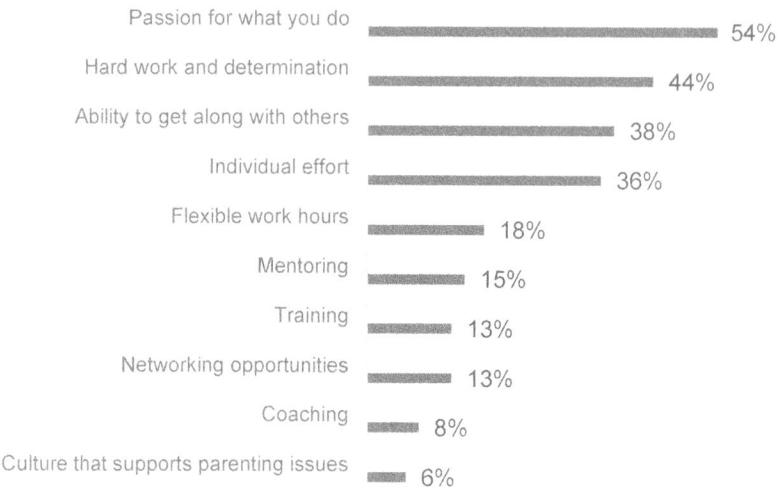

IN SUPPORT OF MY CAREER SUCCESS, I WOULD LIKE MY COMPANY TO OFFER ME:

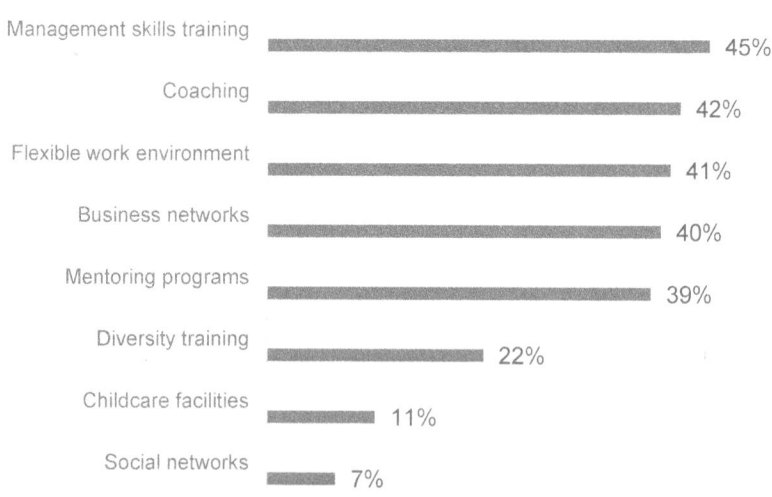

While 88% of respondents were satisfied/very satisfied with the level of success achieved to date, some 24% were unsatisfied with the level of support offered by their employer to achieve success.

The elements that have least contributed to current levels of success are those that are considered vital to future and continued success.

WHAT CAN ORGANISATIONS OFFER?

— Respondents to the survey have their own suggestions as to what can best aid them in furthering their careers and adding value to the organisations for which they work, which provide new confirmation of existing strategies suggested by management and organisational researchers.

— 44.7% would like their employers to offer them management training, which can be reinforced by addressing their stated concerns about targeted planning for skills and management development as a feature of training and development policy and succession planning.

— Related is the desire of 40.4% of respondents for networks to support development, building on the theme of the relational and social nature of women's approach to work.

THE WOMEN AND SUCCESS PARADOX

The factors that we class as supporting and growing factors were seen as the least contributing to current levels of success.

— Mentoring, coaching and training

— Networking opportunities

— Culture that supports parenting issues.

When asked what factors brought even greater success, women first looked to these factors.

— Management skills training

— Coaching

— Flexible working environment

— Business networks

— Mentoring.

What would be possible if these factors were present initially?

If you don't know where you are going any road can take you there.

Lewis Carroll

CH.4 NEEDS

We all have needs. I invite you to think of needs as neither good nor bad—they are what they are: things we need.

Needs change, as does the intensity of those needs. When you were younger, you may have had a need to be liked? This may or may not be a need for you now. Suspend judgement.

A place to explore is how your needs are currently being met. Are you consciously meeting your needs in a positive way? Or are your needs being expressed in a negative and potentially more damaging way? Until we become conscious and aware fully of our needs and how we are fulfilling those needs, we can fall into the trap of having those needs met in ways that don't serve us or others.

CASE STUDY: SARAH

Sarah was a successful senior director in a multinational financial institution with a reporting line of over 7,000 people. She was driven; she cared deeply for the work she did; she maintained a solid social network; and she was close to her family.

During our coaching sessions, Sarah would often speak of feeling unworthy. She would beat herself up and couldn't understand why or from where this stemmed. She acknowledged her successful career and that she was fortunate to have good friends and a good life.

As our sessions progressed a pattern emerged; however, we still hadn't uncovered the core of what was driving her feelings of unworthiness and not feeling good enough. There was a punishing aspect to how Sarah viewed herself at times.

Sarah was a healthy, creative and resourceful person. There was nothing to fix—nothing was broken. She recognised that she was doing well in life and in her career, and she was genuinely mystified about why she would succumb, at times, to intense feelings of self-loathing.

At one of our sessions she put her head in her hand and said, 'I can't believe that I have done this again. It's just so embarrassing. The walk into the office on the Monday morning is torturous'.

Sarah would often join her colleagues for Friday night drinks after work. There was a heavy drinking culture, and after a few drinks Sarah would be dancing on the tables; doing her best rendition of a pole dancer; and in her words, 'pick up some cute bloke and take him home'. She was feeling distraught.

The bar was close to the office. Any number of people from work—friends or those who reported to her, or management—may have been there. And worse still, for Sarah, one of them may have been the one with whom she spent the night.

Evidently this was a difficult topic for Sarah to explore; however, I asked her what it was that upset her most about her behaviour. While it took courage to confront her issues, the payoff for doing so was incredibly valuable and long lasting.

Sarah explained that she felt anxious the whole weekend and would dread walking into her office on Monday morning. She would relive that Friday night over and over, trying to figure out who was with her at the bar and how this would impact her reputation. She would reprimand herself throughout the weekend: telling herself off for *being stupid* and for *doing this again*.

It took immense courage for Sarah to confront this part of her life; to deal with how it was impacting her, and to take action to change it. It wasn't about Sarah's decision of how she spent her Friday nights, for her it was about the negative spiral of self-loathing she would endure the entire weekend.

I became curious about the need that was driving Sarah. Why did she continue to engage in a pattern of behaviour and choices that would cause her such distress?

I asked Sarah to work through an exercise (The Needs Exercise, page 51) that would help her to explore her needs; to look deeply at what was important about meeting those needs; how those needs were currently being met; and what was the impact when those needs were not met.

Through her investment, courage and dedication to the task, Sarah began to understand herself and her drivers. She was able to choose a new way of behaving, and she began to reprogram how she would spent her weekends. She also addressed what thoughts and beliefs dominated her.

Through this process Sarah realised that she loved performing—singing and dancing in public was something that she loved to do. *She uncovered a need to perform.* This surprised her as she had never formally attended acting or singing classes and hadn't been in any plays or productions since school days. However, when she told her family and friends that she was interested in performing they weren't in the least bit surprised.

Sarah had uncovered a need that she realised she was meeting in an unhealthy way; she swapped the table tops of bars for a stage and joined an amateur dramatic society. (It was a pleasure to watch her play the lead in a musical six months later.)

Sarah had uncovered a need and a way to express it more positively, which also provided the basis for some deeper discoveries and positive changes.

By now having her need to perform in public expressed in a healthier way, Sarah stopped dancing on tables in the local bar. She made conscious choices about how—and where—she invested in her social time. She set some boundaries between work and social activities, and she reassessed her lifestyle choices, and her health and well-being. This resulted in improved self-esteem and reputation, and she spent her weekends enjoying herself rather than beating herself up.

The process for Sarah wasn't about her choices surrounding alcohol (however, a shift also happened here) and how she spent her time. She still chose to socialise and have relationships but she now chose to place some boundaries around how and where she did this—thus removing the need for self-loathing afterwards.

Next we worked on Sarah's beliefs, the behaviours that supported those beliefs and the outcome of those behaviours.

She identified a voice that spoke to her regularly. She identified a dialogue that she was running and realised that it supported a belief that she had carried since childhood. A voice that belonged to someone else; a person from her past, who from an early age, told her she wasn't good enough. She was now able to view this voice from the perspective of the adult she was and she choose not to buy into its message. Sarah decided to show some love and compassion for her younger self; to let go of the belief that hailed from someone else; and to stop allowing it to drive her behaviours and choices as an adult.

The Needs Exercise

The following *Needs Exercise* was given to me many years ago by Blaire Palmer[3], a wonderful coach who worked with me after the sale of my business.

The Needs Exercise is the exercise that Sarah worked though. What made it powerful for her—and for 1000s of other clients who have invested in doing this exercise—was that she took time to work through each need, revisiting the exercise again and again over a 3–6-month period. This is an exercise of discovery—a gift that keeps on giving.

Here's how to maximise this powerful exercise:

1. Look through all the words in the following table. Circle everything that resonates with you as a *need*. There is no limit to how many you circle. Clients often call me when doing this exercise saying that they have circled most of the sheet. This is normal; there is no set number of needs. It is unique to you.

2. Take notice of what pushes any buttons. If you are absolutely convinced that, in no way, this is a need for you, circle it and have a deeper look.

3. You may find yourself laughing as a need resonates with you—circle it.

---

[3] Blaire trained with Coach U.

4. For any need that is neutral and has no impact on you, move on. It's possibly not a need for you.

For some clients, by diving deeply into what they need and how they meet their needs has often brought about lightbulb moments, insights, positive results and surprises—I wish the same for you.

Once you have circled all the needs look at the questions at the end of the chart and answer each one for every need circled.

Take your time to invest in the process by answering all three questions at the end of the table. Each question has a question(s) within it; take time to look at all of them individually.

BE ACCEPTED	Approved–Included–Respected–Permitted–Popular–Sanctioned–Cool–Allowed–Tolerated
TO ACCOMPLISH	Achieve–Fulfil–Realise–Reach–Profit–Attain Yield–Consummate–Victory
BE ACKNOWLEDGED	Worthy–Praised–Honoured–Flattered–Complimented–Appreciated–Valued–Thanked
WORK	Career–Performance–Vocation–Press, push–Make it happen–A task–Responsibility–Industriousness–Busy
RECOGNITION	Noticed–Remembered–Known–Regarded–Credit–Acclaim–Heeded–Seen–Celebrated
SAFETY	Security–Protected–Stable–Fully informed–Deliberate–Vigilant–Cautious–Alert–Guarded
ORDER	Perfection–Symmetry–Consistent–Sequential–Checklists–Unvarying–Right-ness–Literal-ness–Regulated

POWER	Authority–Capacity–Results–Omnipotence–Strength–Might–Stamina–Prerogative–Influence
BE COMFORTABLE	Luxury–Opulence–Excess–Prosperity–Indulgence–Abundance–Not work–Taken care of–Served
PEACE	Quietness–Calmness–Unity–Reconciliation–Stillness–Balance–Agreements–Respite–Steadiness
BE LOVED	Liked–Cherished–Esteemed–Held fondly–Be desired–Be preferred–Be relished–Be adored–Be touched
BE RIGHT	Correct–Not mistaken–Honest–Morally right–Be deferred to–Be confirmed–Be advocated–Be encouraged–Understood
DUTY	Obligated–Do the right thing–Follow–Obey–Have a task–Satisfy others–Prove self–Be devoted–Have a cause
BE FREE	Unrestricted–Privileged–Immune–Independent–Autonomous–Sovereign–Not obligated–Self-reliant–Liberated

TO COMMUNICATE	Be heard–Gossip–Tell stories–Make a point–Share–Talk–Be listened to–Comment–Informed
BE CARED FOR	Get attention–Be helped–Cared about–Be saved–Be attended to–Be treasured–Tenderness–Get gifts–Embraced
CERTAINTY	Clarity–Accuracy–Assurance–Obviousness–Guarantees–Promises–Commitments–Exactness–Precision
TO CONTROL	Dominate–Command–Restrain–Manage–Correct others–Be obeyed–Not ignored–Keep status quo–Restrict
BE NEEDED	Improve others–Be a critical link–Be useful–Be craved–Please others–Affect others–Need to give–Be important–Be material
HONESTY	Forthrightness–Uprightness–No lying–Sincerity–Loyalty–Frankness–No withholds–No perpetrations–Tell all

Here are some questions to ask yourself about your needs:

What is it about this need that makes it important enough to be a personal need? (5 reasons)

1	
2	
3	
4	
5	

Who am I when this need is met? How do I act? What do I think about? What motivates me? (5 things)

1	
2	
3	
4	
5	

Needs

Who am I when this need isn't met? How do I behave? How do I feel about myself? (5 responses)

1	
2	
3	
4	
5	

MASLOW'S ORIGINAL 5 HIERARCHY OF NEEDS

Investing in understanding what drives your needs will help you to make healthier choices about how you have those needs met.

In 1943, Abraham Maslow, an American psychologist, stated that as human beings we need our most basic needs met before we can move up the hierarchy towards our higher needs. His hierarchy of needs originally included five levels, to which in later years, he added three more.

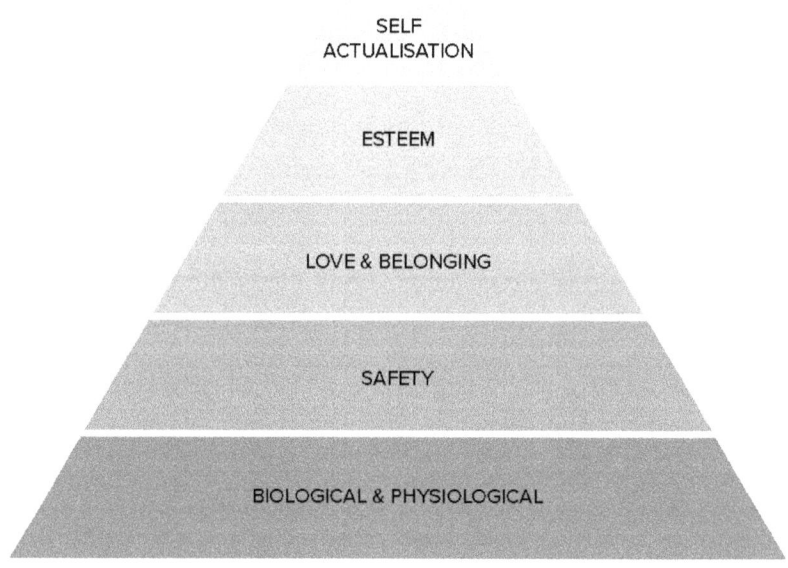

FIGURE 1: MASLOW'S 5 HIERARCHY OF NEEDS

5 HIERARCHY OF NEEDS

1. Biological and physiological: this included basic needs of food and drink, shelter and warmth, sex, sleep.
2. Safety: security and protection, stability, order.

3. Love and belonging: intimacy, friendship, love.
4. Esteem: self-esteem, achievement, status, independence.
5. Self-actualisation: realising personal potential, self-fulfilment, personal growth.

We are motivated by what we need, beginning with our most basic needs, which evolved as humankind has evolved.

It is valuable to reflect upon Maslow's research to help us to understand how our needs influence our lives.

Reflect back to the needs exercise and where your needs fall into Maslow's 'Hierarchy of Needs'. This may help you to create order in your list of what to focus on when examining how to begin to get your needs met in a healthy way.

People are like stained-glass windows. They sparkle and shine when the sun is out, but when the darkness sets in their true beauty is revealed only if there is light from within.

Elisabeth Kübler-Ross

CH.5 BELIEFS

Beliefs are powerful. What we believe has a profound impact on our health and wellbeing. It directs our behaviours, drives the results and shapes our lives. We create our lives from what we believe to be true.

What is a belief?

Peter Halligan (2005), a psychologist at Cardiff University defined belief as, 'A belief is a mental architecture of how we interpret the world'.

The Oxford Dictionary defines belief as, 'an acceptance that something exists or is true, especially one without proof'.

We form beliefs from an early age based on our understanding and surrounding circumstances. These beliefs shape our world. Think about the beliefs you hold true in your life. Get conscious about your beliefs and how these beliefs form the basis of the script that is your life.

Your life script is based on your beliefs, often unconsciously; collect the evidence to reinforce these beliefs and further entrench them into your psyche to shape your experiences and life.

Dr Eric Berne, a Canadian-born psychiatrist best known as the creator of Transactional Analysis and the author of *Games People Play*, introduced the concept of life scripts (Scripts Analysis) in his research and work. Berne said,

> Script Analysis is the method of uncovering the early decisions, made unconsciously, as to how life shall be lived.

> The purpose of script analysis is to help a person achieve autonomy by recognising the script's influence on their thoughts and actions by creating awareness and consciousness, which ultimately allows a person to decide whether to keep running this script or abandon it.

I invite you to do the same. Think about the scripts you are running and the beliefs that underpin them. The goal is to achieve more freedom and a life of ease and grace that allows space for more opportunities, more fun and more success.

Dr Berne described someone who is autonomous as being 'script free' and a 'real person'.

Scripts, like patterns of behaviour are completely within our control. We can manage and change our scripts. The first step is to uncover the scripts that you are running and the behaviours that enforce these scripts making them true.

Uncovering the beliefs that anchor you to your world, which create your scripts is a worthy investment of your time. I invite you to approach this exploration—like all explorations—with a deep curiosity that helps to keep judgement and self-criticism at bay.

If I haven't yet managed to convince you to do this work—to invest in yourself—then let me add some more incentives. The world of new biology [4] (also known as molecular biology), neuroscience and mind/body health boast new discoveries and further understanding of the link between our beliefs and how these beliefs impact us at an emotional and cellular level. These discoveries also secure a link between our beliefs and our health and wellbeing, and the lives we

---

[4] See glossary

currently live. We manifest our lives by our thoughts, our beliefs, our behaviours and our actions.

Dr Bruce H Lipton (2007), a prominent former medical-school professor and research scientist, explores this in greater detail, which he shares in his ground-breaking book *The Biology of Belief*. His research into how cells receive and process information is radically changing our understanding of life. He proposes that genes and DNA may not control our biology but rather DNA is controlled by signals from outside our cells, which include the energetic messages emanating from positive and negative thoughts.

Dr Lipton is not the first to suggest that our health, whether physical or mental, is significantly impacted by our thoughts that stem from our beliefs, nor that we can change our health for the better if we retrain our thinking.

He is among the academics, scientists and medical professionals helping to provide evidence to support this theory.

What does this mean for you?

How is this an incentive to invest in you and your success?

If beliefs are the core that contribute to our health and wellbeing, I believe that uncovering our core beliefs and consciously choosing and challenging them is integral to a fulfilled and satisfied life—a life that we are proud to live, a life with no regrets and a life in which we can feel successful.

We either make ourselves miserable or we make ourselves strong. The amount of work is the same.

Carlos Castaneda

CH.6 LIMITING BELIEFS

CASE STUDY: DIANA

Diana worked for a leading national company that was undergoing a large scale change. With this change came many opportunities to step up, be more visible and to impact strategy and direction.

Diana felt she wasn't able to maximise the opportunities available and attributed this to a combination of the environment and culture of the organisation and her own approach. She wanted me to help her work on how she could shift this dynamic and how she could get better results at work, be more visible and become a key, trusted advisor in her department from whom others would seek advice.

She felt undermined at work, that her senior colleagues didn't treat her seriously and that her opinion wasn't valued. Her days would end in self–doubt, frustration and anger. The cause of this was largely due to her performance in meetings—in particular, meetings that involved senior members of the organisation.

She felt she couldn't get a word in and when she did, she wasn't having the impact that she wanted. Frustration would ensue when she failed to contribute something that was then contributed by another team member. She became so anxious about the meetings that her focus was entirely on herself and her performance, which resulted in her missing vital information, both spoken and unspoken.

At the beginning of our work together, Diana's focus was the culture of the organisation. She felt it was hierarchical and didn't allow for the voice of someone in a less senior role. She felt that her opinion wasn't valued and she really didn't know why she was being asked to attend the meetings. She put it down to her boss being overstretched so she would be sent to attend in his place.

There was pattern of blame and avoidance in her approach that warranted a deeper look.

I asked Diana to share her beliefs about this situation. She believed that, 'I am only there because my boss can't attend. My opinion isn't valued'.

As we explored this deeper Diana uncovered a core belief that she had been running for a very long time. That belief was *I'm not good enough. What I say doesn't matter.*

Those beliefs drove her behaviour and those behaviours impacted results and how she was perceived.

We worked through the beliefs exercise below, which helped her to provide insight into the core beliefs she held; how those beliefs impacted how she behaved and the outcomes on her life.

With her permission I have shared Diana's template with you.

LIMITING BELIEF

I'm only there because my boss can't attend.

My opinion isn't valued.

BEHAVIOUR

I asked Diana how she behaved when she believed this to be true. We needed to focus in on her behaviours: what does she see when she believes this. The key to this exercise is to focus and drill down on behaviours.

Behaviour: Defensive: I sulked and held back. I stayed silent in meetings and got angry when someone raised a point I had thought of but didn't voice. Combative: ready for a fight. Resistant. Obstructive. Scowling, resulting in short abrupt answers.

OUTCOME

We moved on to exploring the outcomes of her behaviours.

Outcome: Loss of confidence: I didn't demonstrate my value or expertise. I limited my opportunities and weakened my personal brand/reputation. I most certainly missed opportunities and often lost the thread of what was going on in meetings. I isolated myself and damaged relationships with people who were in more senior positions—in particular, my relationship with my boss.

Women and Success

The next step was to invite Diana to play a game. I asked her what she thought was the complete opposite of the limiting belief she held.

The belief she chose was, 'My opinion is valued *and* valuable'.

We switched this to an 'I' message and dropped this belief into the template below. I asked Diana to stand up, to try on the belief, and to move to the other side of the table. I asked her to imagine what it would be like to hold this belief as true. Standing up and changing location is an important part of this exercise, as it helps to shift the energy and perspective of the limiting belief.

BELIEF

I am invited to the meeting. I have value to add.

My opinion is valued.

I explained to Diana that, at this point, it really did not matter whether or not she was able to hold this belief as true, we were just playing.

BEHAVIOUR

I asked Diana to think about what behaviours she would see if this was a belief that she held as true.

Behaviour: I would speak up more, be less defensive. (Whenever Diana stated something in the *negative* like, *be less defensive*, we flipped it to its *positive* counterpart. *Less defensive* was flipped to, *more open, more positive body language*.) I could see happier, more positive behaviour: Diana was smiling.

Highlighting this to Diana and drawing her attention to her posture was an important part of the process.

OUTCOME

We dug deep to discover the outcomes of these behaviours.

Outcome: I would feel like I had contributed. More satisfaction. Developing more presence and a stronger reputation. Participating and adding value. Better results for my team and department. Ultimately, better business decisions for the company when everyone is participating, including me. Increased confidence and satisfaction. Feeling valued; like I am making a contribution. More options about the future within the company

The list grew, as did Diana's positivity.

The key to this process is not to work hard at changing your beliefs, or focusing on the outcomes you desire—this works for some people but is wasn't working for Diana. She had tried many times to focus on changing her belief or focusing solely on the results she wanted. She wasn't getting results doing this and needed another approach.

I asked Diana if she was able to control her behaviours. She felt confident that she could. We can always control how we behave and this is where I invited her to focus.

I invited her to focus on these behaviours in conjunction with the desired beliefs, to implement these in her meetings, and to be mindful of her impact both physically and verbally. To smile, sit up straight and to contribute.

I received an excited phone call a few weeks later from Diana. The meetings she once attended with dread were now meetings that she attended with confident. She was able to contribute in a meaningful way now that she had **got out of her own way**.

At the end of the meeting, one of the senior managers stopped to talk to me, he said that he liked my suggestions and approach to the issues and that he was pleased that I was now attending the meetings. I was shocked as I had been attending these meeting for six months. I had made myself invisible. Fortunately, I am now visible.

This is how women self-sabotage and self-destruct. Unless we have constant witnesses to our hard work, we are convinced we pull off every day of our lives through smoke and mirrors.

Sarah Ban Breathnach

She lacks confidence, she craves admiration insatiably. She lives on the reflections of herself in the eyes of others. She does not dare to be herself.

Anais Nin

CH.7 SELF-SABOTAGE:

THE SUCCESS TERMINATOR

Self-sabotage is the not-so-silent assassin that lurks in the shadows of our psyche. It waits for moments of doubt and weakness to emerge and extinguish the flame of our potential. It has many names: The Inner Critic, The Saboteur and The Silent Assassin are some of the more commonly referred to titles. They need little sustenance and thrive in a system of self-doubt creating a ripple effect in our lives and the lives of those with whom we interact.

Our saboteurs keep us stuck and small.

If you google self-sabotage you will get over 17,000 results dedicated to it. It's like a bad reality TV show: we want to ignore it, but it's everywhere showcasing and highlighting the stars, themes and dramas of the show. Like any production there can be a cast of thousands. Self-sabotage has many names and a tribe of cronies colluding with each other fighting for the spotlight.

Self-sabotage has sophisticated PR agents; a dedicated team to ensure its prominence and dominance. It can be impossible to escape the hype, attention and publicity. No wonder we allow this phenomenon to derail our best intentions and hopes.

We may not consciously tune in to its broadcasts, often taking a stand and saying, 'Hey, I don't watch that rubbish,' but its sheer reach and presence holds us in its grip. We hear The Saboteur's messages whispering conspiratorially to us, usually when we are at our most vulnerable.

Self-sabotage, like those B-grade reality shows, loves attention, and the more we give it, the more it thrives. Like any parasitic relationship, its survival derails us both physically and emotionally. It sets you up to fail, so sometimes you don't even try. And when you do try and fail, it grabs you in its embrace soothing you, telling you it tried to warn you. It makes failure your enemy when in reality to fail is to learn (failure can be your friend). Ask any scientist if you need validation of this.

The messages that your saboteur whispers sounds like this:

— Oh no, I can't do that.
— Who do I think I am?
— I don't have the right qualifications/experience.
— Stop, it's dangerous. I'll only get hurt if I try.

Of course, we know deep down that self-sabotage isn't an entity that lurks within us nor a voice that invades our minds. It is part of our mindset; it is a part of us. The first step in any recovery is awareness—acknowledgement that the problem lies within and the only way to move forward is to do the work.

The voice of The Saboteur is **our** voice.

Sometimes it's helpful to understand the origin of this voice, the timeline of when it appeared and from where—sometimes it's not. We can get trapped in the void of saboteur analysis feeding blame and anger, and in the process we nourish our saboteur as it morphs into many sophisticated guises. Our saboteurs are clever and have many faces and voices. Their evolution and reproduction is swift and ever changing. It can be exhausting keeping up.

The most important step is to recognise the voice and to choose consciously what you take from it and what power you will give it.

Think back over your life and identify the times that self-sabotage won and stopped you from achieving the opportunities, desires and adventures you wanted.

— In what areas of your life does *the voice* show up most frequently and most loudly?
— What does a typical conversation sound like?
— What is the lie that your saboteur would most like you to believe about yourself?

Think of one time when The Saboteur was a great help to you.

I invite you to look at self-sabotage through the lens of curiosity. It's not good or evil, *it is what it i*s. It's a part of us, developed through childhood to adulthood. Many psychologists believe that self-sabotage grew from a place of self-care, a way of protecting us from harm. If you are about to jump off a bridge, which will almost certainly result in injury or death, a voice screaming out, 'you can't do that,' is a valuable voice to hear and to which to pay attention. The problem comes when we allow this voice to remain an unfiltered voice—one of dominance, which keeps us safe, in our comfort zone and away from our potential.

I was first introduced to the concept of self-sabotage while training as a coach more than 15 years ago, through the required reading of Richard D Carson's book *Taming your Gremlin* (2003). This book changed my world; developed my understanding of this concept; and provided valuable strategies for dealing with self-sabotage. I highly recommended *Taming your Gremlin*—it's a fabulous resource.

Carson asks us to begin to recognise the message of The Gremlin, to acknowledge it and give it something else to do so that it doesn't dominate—to see The Gremlin as a *narrator in your head*. 'Simply noticing requires effort, it does not require strain,' says Carson. I love this observation. Noticing and identifying your saboteur need not be an arduous task. If you think this sounds like hard work and you are lining up the excuses why not to invest in this, please know that it is a lot easier than you think and the excuses not to invest may be being streamed by your saboteur.

The key is to remember that the voice of The Saboteur is not to necessarily sabotage—sabotage is the unwitting result. At some point, this voice may have saved you from doing potentially harmful and foolish things.

Acknowledging the role of The Saboteur is a great place to start. Develop an internal script that may sound something like this: *Thank you for your concern, for wanting to protect me.*

This is the point where you are free to choose. Remember all the resources you now have in your life, your skills and your achievements. Take all of this into account when you decide upon the best course of action *for you* and from which voice you will launch action.

This is the point where you are free to choose, no longer ruled by The Saboteur's voice.

THE SABOTEUR'S CONVENTION

Just when you have identified and coded your saboteurs, and are implementing strategies to manage them, they get lonely and seek out the company of their tribe. This is when your saboteurs get locked into dialogue with other people's saboteurs creating a spiral of hilarity and misery. They gather, and feast on your fears by conspiring to divert and derail you. This party is not to celebrate you, its purpose is to keep you stuck—while your saboteurs and their comrades, on the other hand, are having a ball.

When Ellen arrived for her session she burst into laughter while sharing her journey to unmask her saboteurs. 'I got into a massive fight with my husband, it was getting out of control when I suddenly burst out laughing. I realised that *my* saboteurs were having an argument with *his* saboteurs. This made me realise that I have friendships that are based on the mutual enablement of our saboteurs.'

This is not unusual. 'Misery loves company,' is a well-known saying by botanist John Ray (1627–1705). Like misery, self-sabotage is very skilful at finding allies to support its cause.

THE LOYAL SOLDIER

My good friend Rebecca Ryan introduced me to the work of Bill Plotkin (2003) and the concept of The Loyal Soldier from his book *Soulcraft*. This is another lens through which to view self-sabotage, and I felt it was important to share this viewpoint with you.

Similar to the role of The Saboteur, The Loyal Soldier's role is to provide protection to our inner child that has experienced trauma or was wounded in some way. Part of the soldier's duties results in creating rules by which to live in order to ensure protection and shield us from further traumatic situations. Bill Plotkin's defines The Loyal Soldier as '… a courageous, wise, and stubborn sub-personality that formed during our childhood and created a variety of strategies to help us survive the realities (often dysfunctional) of our families and culture'.

In his book, Plotkin examines the manner in which the Japanese government and communities helped post World War II servicemen integrate back into society after many years marooned on islands where they continued to live and survive believing that the war was still being fought. They continued in the disciplines of being a solider, of the serve and protect mindset. When they were found many years later, the Japanese government thought carefully about how to integrate them back into a world. They had been living in peace for many years and were in the process of healing and moving forward. The soldiers needed help to re-enter society and to move beyond their 'loyal soldier' identity.

They were welcomed with public celebration, and were acknowledged for their sacrifice and service—to the people of Japan and to his country. Here is Fr Richard Rohr's explanation:

> After this was done at great length, an elder would stand and announce with authority something to this effect: "The war is now over! The community needs you to let go of what has served you and served us well up to now. The community needs you to return as a man, a citizen, and something beyond a soldier." In our men's work, we call this process "discharging your loyal soldier." This kind of closure is much needed for most of us at the end of all major transitions in life.

To what rules, that your loyal soldiers have created, are you holding on?

Use the power of ritual and celebration to slay sabotage, to thank your loyal soldiers for their service and tell them 'the war is over'.

What I love is that this process comes from a place of honouring the service done—this frees up judgement and criticism. It provides closure which is valuable when transitioning from one development phase to another. It reduces the energy required to manage self-sabotage enabling us to move forward in a healthy and productive way.

IT'S OUR JOB TO MANAGE OUR SELF-SABOTAGE

I'm a huge fan of Sheryl Sandberg's (2013) book *Lean In* where she talks about the internal and external barriers that hold women back from achieving their professional goals. Sandberg says these barriers are rarely deliberated with the focus of discussion being largely on inequalities in the workplace, and how hard it would be to have a career *and* a family. 'I rarely heard anything, however, about the ways I might hold myself back.'

What I love about her book is the call to self-accountability as well as the honesty and vulnerability that she shares with her readers.

One of the ways we hold ourselves back is by ignoring the damage that self-sabotage creates. Implementing strategies to minimise the power and impact of our self-sabotage is one of the many ways that we can blast some of the internal and external barriers that we face as women. It's important for me to note that this issue is not gender specific; men also experience the same blocks that self-sabotage deliver.

Decide right now if a life lived scripted by your self-sabotage is acceptable to you?

Commit to living a life free of the restraints of The Saboteur and move towards a happier, more fulfilled life by minimising stress, creating space for more love, more opportunities, more challenges, more joy and more energy. Stop expending energy on thoughts that undermine and drain you.

Once we understand that we can't eradicate our negative sabotaging thoughts, we are on our way to rehabilitation and a life free from its limiting grip. We are then able to accept this as a normal part of the human condition and use the energy otherwise expended in eradication to the better use of employing more positive strategies to move forward.

Use this 5-step action plan to help.

1. Notice The Saboteurs message.
2. Launch your strategies.
3. Seek support.
4. Seek evidence that shows the best of you.
5. Commit to moving forward without your saboteur.

THE SABOTEUR'S CYCLE

The Saboteur's message creates or enforces a belief, resulting in a pattern of behaviour that gives us an outcome. The good news is that by reframing the way we view The Saboteur's message, we can focus on behaviour that is more helpful. Then *we* can influence our beliefs and outcomes. Follow the steps below:

1. Write down all the beliefs that would go with The Saboteurs messages. You know these, they are old friends and may include: *I'm not good enough, smart enough* etc.
2. Now add the behaviours that support these beliefs.

    What behaviours would do you see when you believe these to be true?
3. List down all the outcomes (what you would get if you activated these behaviours).

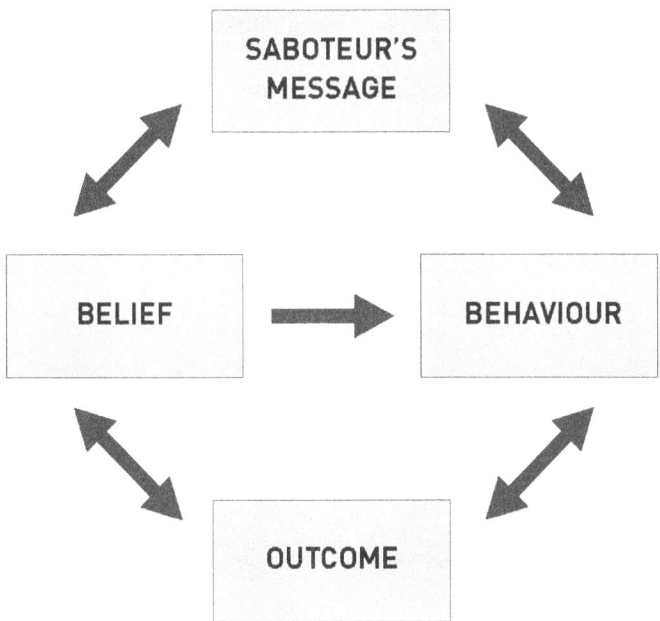

THE CHAMPION

The Champion, our unsung hero, is also within us.

Like The Saboteur, The Champion also wants the best for you, but The Champion operates in a different way. Where The Saboteur is assertive, intrusive, immediately there, invited or not, The Champion frequently needs to be called. What The Champion gives you is courage, and an unfaltering belief in you, your talents, and your ability, your capacity to excel and persevere. The Champion is also the one with the courage to tell you the truth. This is an infallible inner voice that will not only speak when asked, but will speak the truth whatever the consequences. This truth comes from the heart and it is the truth of true caring for you. Unfortunately, most of us do not know our champion very well and have little experience of having this important part of us present at the time when we really need a champion in our lives.

— When has your champion been present?

— Can you give your champion a name?

— What is one area, in your life right now, where you would like to invite your champion to stand beside you?

— What would The Champion say to you?[5]

---

[5] Source: Coaches Training Institute

THE CHAMPION'S CYCLE

In the same way that The Saboteur's message creates or enforces a belief, or a pattern or behaviour that results in an outcome, so does The Champion's message.

Gather your champion's messages. If you are stuggling to do so, then pretend that you are providing some champion messages for your best friend. Follow these steps:

1. Write down all the beliefs that would go with your champions messages. It's OK, you don't have to believe in them, just write them down.
2. Now add the behaviours that support these beliefs. What behaviours would you see if you acted as if these beliefs were true?
3. List down all the outcomes.

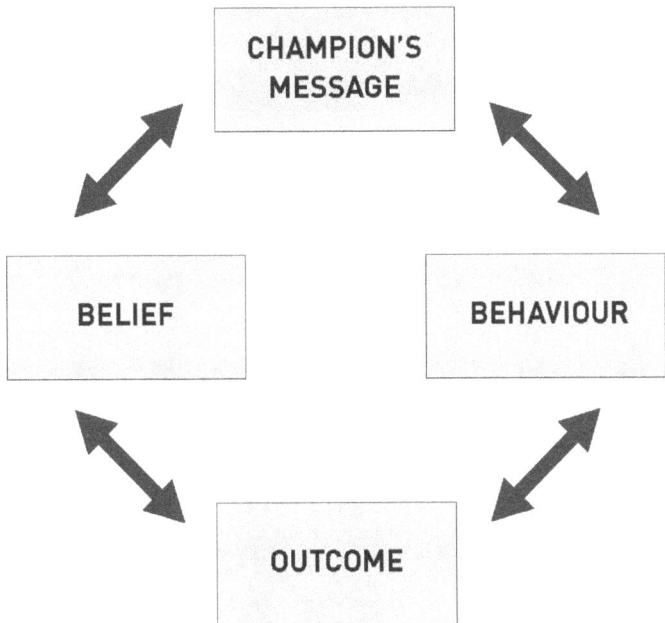

Understanding the land in which you choose to live, will go a long way to helping you understand your drivers, motivators and derailers. Here is one more exercise to help with this important work of discovery.

The Lands Exercise

Imagine your life as country, a land in which you live. Visualise this country, take in the landscape, the enviroment and the climate. You may want to draw the image that you see.

Write down as much as you can about this country. Here are some questions to help you along:

1. What is the climate?
2. Who lives here? Describe them.
3. What is accepted here?
4. What is not accepted?
5. What are the laws that must be obeyed?
6. What happens when these laws are broken?
7. Who enforces these laws?
8. If you were in power, what would you keep?
9. If you were in power, what would you discard?

_____
_____
_____
_____
_____
_____
_____
_____
_____

Now sketch out the country in which your champion lives.

Use the questions and process above as a guide.

Once you have completed this process, ask yourself the following:

1. What are the differences in the two lands?
2. What are the similiarties?
3. Where is there possible conflict between the two lands?
4. Where is there alignment?

_____

_____

_____

_____

Once completed, reflect on the key insights that this process has given you.

Pedestals are for statues, not people.

Debra Munn

Curiouser and curiouser.

Lewis Carroll

We like to put people on a pedestal, give them one character trait, and if they step outside of that shrine like area that we blocked out for them, then we will punish them.

Madonna Ciccone

CH.8 MISERY OR JOY:

HOW DO YOU WANT TO LIVE?

There are two paths in life: misery or joy. Both are valid human experiences. Get conscious about which one you *are* living and which one you *want* to live.

If it's misery you want – then go for it. There are lots of ways to ensure more misery, more unhappiness, and more dissatisfaction.

How are you currently inviting misery into your life? What choices are you making? What dialogue are you running? If you want more misery: just keep doing what you are doing; ramp it up a few notches to maximise the experience.

If it's joy that you seek (my preference), then there are equally as many ways to ensure you experience more joy in your life. How do you currently invite joy into your life? It might be the simple things like going for a walk along the beach (one of my favourite things to do) or appreciating beauty in nature and the people around you. It may be a hobby or sport that keeps you feeling alive. Or stretching yourself, learning. Maybe it's being in the service of others, bringing happiness and joy to the people in your world and beyond. It may be a collection of things. Joy isn't a linear or binary experience, it's like a kaleidoscope offering different combinations, beauty and changing landscapes. Life, like joy, isn't stagnant, it moves and grows as we move and grow.

Begin by becoming aware of your chosen path. You may not be consciously aware of your choice. When our conscious choices aren't aligned with behaviours that support us and bring us closer to what we want: we need to look deeper.

A choice has been made. Bring this choice to your conscious mind, look at it get curious.

The good news is that you can choose to either keep this choice or choose differently. Just get conscious; do it now. Choose which path you would like to live.

The Misery or Joy Exercise

Take a moment to write down all the behaviours and actions that bring you closer to living a joyful life, and all the behaviours that take you away from living joyfully.

_____

_____

_____

_____

_____

_____

CONSCIOUSLY CHOOSING JOY

Life feels more aligned and balanced when you make a conscious choice to live joyfully. Your focus will be a deep gratitude for what you have, not for what you don't have.

There are many examples in life and history of people who have made this choice and who have achieved happiness, lived fulfilled lives, and achieves remarkable things. Regardless of their life circumstances, they propel themselves forward and show up in the world fully. They can't help but do the work they were meant to do—to fulfil their purpose and live a life filled with joy.

That doesn't mean that they don't experience challenges, have off days and sometimes want to throw in the towel. They are human, just like you. They have made choices, just like you. However, what they do have is a deep connection to what's important to them, to who they are prepared to be, what they are prepared to tolerate and what they will not.

They are clear about boundaries and what they will not allow or accept into their lives, and they take action to enforce these boundaries—which as you know can be challenging at times.

A clarity emerges when you become fierce about what you *will not* accept. Rick Tamlyn (2013), my friend and author of *Play your Bigger Game* talks about your 'no not that'.

Your *no not that* is what you are fierce about *not* accepting in your life, you stand strongly for this and regardless of the fear that you may have or be experiencing in your life, you move into action because you truly believe that this is needed. Your excuses about not acting are drowned out by your conviction and passion. You are 100% clear about what you will and will not accept or tolerate. This propels you towards your purpose, it reminds you why you are doing this and what's important about it, which in turn keeps the excuses, fear and apathy at bay.

I faced *no not that* when I made the decision to sell my share of The Company I had built, then my home, and move back to Australia after 17 years in London. I was fearful about my future: what would I do? What would I become? However, deep down I knew that if I stayed in the business—an option that was available to me—it would destroy me. This was a strong feeling. If I remained where I was and living my life the way I was living it, I would suffer dire consequences. It did not make sense, and yet I knew this to be true. I also believed that staying would unravel and damage the business, and in doing so would impact others who depended on the business for their livelihood and careers

It all sounds rather dramatic, doesn't it? Yet for me this held truth, and the fear of that was ultimately greater than the fear of such significant change. I connected strongly with my *no not that*: I would not let that happen to myself or to others. I took the only option. I got into action and began the long process of extracting myself from the life that I had built around me – that which had provided a safe container for over 10 years. I worked through my issues and started making positive steps towards a new life and career.

INTRODUCING ALICE COLES (AND THE BAYVIEW CITIZENS FOR SOCIAL JUSTICE)

Alice Coles is a remarkable lady. I was introduced to Alice's story through Rick Tamlyn and his work with bringing The Bigger Game to the world.

Alice had a strong connection to her *no not that,* which propelled her into action for herself, her beliefs, and what she valued and for her community, in order to create a better life.

It began in 1994, when the state of Virginia planned to build a maximum-security prison less than a mile from the neighbourhood school. Alice said, *no not that.* She was not going to allow the state of Virginia to build that prison. Alice was firmly grounded in her values; she was deeply connected to her heritage and community.

With only a high-school education and a job handpicking meat out of crabs, Alice emerged as the strongest voice driving social change for her and her fellow residents in Bayview. Her actions and leadership led to Bayview's positive redevelopment into a strong community of people with a lifetime commitment to better living.

'I never believed in this lifetime that I would actually live like people,' reported a Bayview resident.[6]

Alice took action. She didn't allow the fact that she had never lobbied, or performed any public speaking to stop her from achieving her goals. She looked at the gaps in her skill set and knowledge, and took action by educating herself about the Department of

---

[6] All quotes in this piece are from a 60 Minutes interview (2003).

Corrections. The pattern of education and learning would continue as she strove to achieve a goal that was bigger than one person.

In Rick Tamlyn's words, 'She became a Bigger Game Player'.

Alice rallied and gained support from within her community. Something powerful had begun: a shift was occurring around what people would accept in their lives and what they would not.

Alice had not only connected to her *no not that*, she connected into the *no not that* of her community. She rallied and spoke publically to galvanise support and momentum.

They fought the proposal for the prison and won. 'We decided to fight it,' Coles recalls, 'because we didn't have anywhere to go and we didn't have anything to lose'.

Alice didn't have a lot of the resources—those that others enjoy, take advantage of and leverage from. She didn't boast the opportunity of extended education; and she didn't have the budget and resources of corporate-world professionals.

There were no leadership development programs, public speaking courses or other types of formal education and development programs. She didn't say, *I need to do this before I can do something about the issue*. She got into action and while in action did all she could to continue to develop and educate herself in service of achieving her goals.

Alice became the most powerful voice and force for transforming her community. She connected into the community's desire to 'live like people' and created a movement for social justice and change. She empowered herself and others through her choice, and she most certainly moved toward more joy in her life.

After the prison triumph, Alice said, 'Well if we could defeat a prison, what else could we do?'

This propelled her into her next challenge, which would transform her life and the lives of the citizens of Bayview.

What Alice and her community were willing to accept had changed.

'People looked at how they were living. They lived in a type of squalor that most Americans would like to believe no longer exists.'

The people of Bayview—under the leadership of Alice Coles—connected more deeply to their *no not that*. They were no longer prepared to live in poverty. They looked how they contributed to this through acceptance and began to dream of a better life.

They began to dream about living like people.

'It was like a dream. The people dreamed big,' said Cozzie Lockwood, a founder of The Bayview Citizens for Social Justice. 'Especially when you're poor, you dream big the biggest dream you want. Buy the land across the street, and build over there.

'This was the beginning of the beginning,' says Coles

It would take another 14 years for Alice and her community to gather support and funding. After relentless campaigning, and blasting through blocks and hurdles, Alice Coles and Bayview Citizens for Social Justice, Inc. (BCSJ) raised over $11 million. They purchased the

> prison site which consisted of 104 acres and an additional 54 acres and built a new town of mixed housing and infrastructure.
>
> This gave many Bayview citizens new amenities and luxuries that are considered normal in America, amenities that people of Bayview didn't have like central heating and indoor plumbing. They thought these amenities were part of someone else's life. To this day Alice leads BCSJ as executive director.
>
> My favourite response from Alice, when asked if one person can make a difference was, 'And if I couldn't be the door that opened to a better life, I'll be the hinge to hold the door. So, one person can make a difference. Yes'.

When the changes you need to make feel overwhelming and opening that door to change becomes too hard: what is the hinge that will help you move towards the life of which you dream?

There is a grounding that happens when we consciously choose joy in our life. We seek out joy and make decisions that support joy and fulfilment. This results in more joy in our lives. This happens both consciously and unconsciously; a healthier pattern begins to play out.

Get conscious of the choices and decisions you are making. Ask yourself: will this take me toward joy or further away from it?

How often have you complained about having to do something or attend a social function when you don't really want to go? Or engaging with someone with whom you don't like spending time?

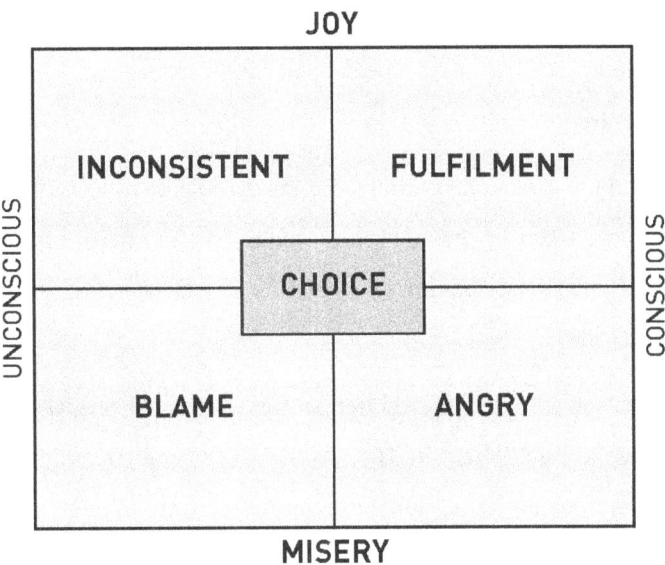

It's easy to fall into the pattern of negativity: collecting and sharing all the reasons why you have to do this. Immersing yourself in complaining and being negative takes you further away from joy.

There may be times that we choose to attend something or do something that we really don't want to do. We are bound by a sense of duty or obligation. Getting clear on what is driving that choice is important.

CASE STUDY: LARA

Lara, a client I worked with many years ago, was a very successful entrepreneur, sought after speaker at conferences, and mentor to aspiring entrepreneurs.

She complained regularly about having to spend time with 'energy suckers': her word for people who drained her. In one of our sessions she complained about having to have dinner with someone with whom she didn't want to spend time.

Her pattern was to put the dinner so far ahead in her diary that she didn't have to think about it. Then as the weeks approached she would become anxious about it, start to complain and put blame firmly onto the other person.

She would dive into self-dialogue that sounded something like this: *It's not fair; I work hard and then have to spend time with these people. It's going to be so tedious.* And on it would go: *why does this always happen to me? I keep attracting these types of people.*

The last statement was a great place for us to explore together. Lara felt safe and was ready to look at why this pattern occurred in her life.

Here's what she discovered through our coaching process.

Lara listed all the people she felt fell into the same category of 'energy suckers'. We began to look more deeply at the pattern and themes that these situations presented. Lara began to see her connection and role in this. She discovered how she contributed to this pattern; how *she* often set up these friendships; and at what point the friendships became difficult for her.

Her insight hit at 3 am one morning; and it hit hard. It wasn't an easy place for her to look. Courage and self-responsibility were necessary for her to take responsibility for her contribution to this dynamic and to move on from this pattern. Lara called me the next day and we got together.

Lara realised that the unhealthy friendships she had collected all began in the same way. She would meet someone and they would be very complimentary about her achievements and quite in awe of her—as a remarkable woman. Lara would joke about being put on a pedestal. She would dispense advice and talk happily about her achievements. 'In the beginning it was fun. I felt special and respected.'

Lara was an incredibly generous person who wanted to help others and found herself in a situation common to many. She has a lot to offer and loves to do so.

As these friendships developed she would feel a shift; she would feel neediness from the other person and wished to pull away from it.

However, she didn't really know how to do this and would start to avoid the other person. When she felt she couldn't continue doing this, she would reluctantly agree to meet. Tension would arise within the friendship and the cracks would get wider—resulting in a confrontation and hurt for all concerned.

Lara felt that once the other person got to know her—as a person, not as the image of who she was in their eyes—she was toppled from the pedestal. And then it would get nasty.

It's a common experience to put people on a pedestal especially when they are in the limelight. This becomes problematic as it is a relationship built on fragile and false foundations. The person on the pedestal may, at first, feel complimented, special and important. Their ego is enjoying the attention; however, as time progresses, feelings of disconnect, and in some cases isolation, begin to kick in.

The person on the pedestal can begin to feel resentful that they are not being seen for who they are, and that the other person's image and expectations of them are unrealistic. This is what happened to Lara. Catch ups with her friend became awkward and strained.

Her friend Helen became critical and judgemental about Lara and the way she lived her life. Whenever Lara showed uncertainty or vulnerability, Helen became irritated. 'I felt like the more I was me the angrier Helen became,' noticed Lara.

Lara had a close circle of great friends where she experienced and participated in healthy friendships. She didn't understand why she kept getting stuck in friendships that drained her.

Through the coaching process Lara was able to unpack the unhealthy friendships in which she found herself by using her current situation with Helen as a case study.

She began to look more deeply at what she was creating in her life and was able to identify a pattern that would help her understand how she got into, collaborated with and encouraged these friendships.

Her 3 am insight came from a question I had posed during her coaching session when she complained first about meeting Helen. I asked Lara about the payback from the friendship: What she was getting from her friendship with Helen? What made their friendship worth it?

Her response was that she was getting nothing from the friendship. I asked her to consider further this enquiry, to keep asking herself what she was getting from the friendship and to write down everything that popped for her. (Lara was getting a need to feel special and acknowledged met in an unhealthy way.)

The first step in this process was for Lara to get clarity on this and take ownership for her contribution to a friendship that wasn't healthy for either of them.

She came to our next session with a very long list: a list that surprised her and caused her a lot of discomfort.

Her list included:

1. I get to help Helen.
2. I get to share what I know.
3. I get to feel superior.
4. I get to feel popular.
5. I get to feel important.

Lara had highlighted two points that she felt were the *key* payback elements for the friendship.

'I get to feel superior.' Lara realised she felt more superior to Helen— a realisation that devastated her at the time. At this point, I want to reiterate that Lara was a loving and caring person, who had many solid and healthy relationships in her life. She wasn't a nasty person who sought out ways to make others feel inferior. Like many people, she found herself in a reoccurring situation until she took positive actions to break the cycle and move into a healthier way of being.

Lara had also identified other similar friendships. In total, there were five friendships in varying stages of decay (as she put it).

She connected deeply with a desire to help others—hence entering into these friendships—and to share what had helped her become successful. She had a genuine desire to be of service to others in this way.

NEXT STEPS

Now that Lara had clarity and understanding of how she developed unhealthy friendships, she felt confident that she would no longer engage, nurture or contribute to these again. And she didn't.

That was 15 years ago. Today Lara continues to thrive in business. She maintains healthy and loving relationships and no longer attracts or develops friendships with people who put her on a pedestal and then pull her down.

I spoke with Lara before including her story in this book; she hopes that through her story others would benefit.

We talked about the situation all those years ago and she had this to say:

> You know back then, when I was in it, it felt so suffocating. I felt a sense of obligation that stifled me. When I realised why I was doing this, that I helped to create these situations, I didn't want to believe it at first. Then I could no longer ignore it. I was devastated and knew I had to do something about it, and with your support was able to. The most uncomfortable thing I have ever done is to end the unhealthy friendships that I had collected in a responsible way. I promised myself that I would never put myself or anyone else in that position again.

Lara took responsibility for her actions and behaviours and changed the landscape for herself going forward. The clincher for her was ending each unhealthy friendship responsibly. She met with Helen and had a courageous and honest conversation. She apologised for her role in their dynamic and said that she would not be continuing with their friendship. Lara then extracted herself from the other five friendships. Having done all that, she was determined never to repeat it.

Next, I have outlined the process that helped Lara develop understanding and insight and move forward positively. Please note that through our coaching sessions, further questions emerged taking Lara's level of understanding to a deeper level.

It may be useful to partner with a trusted friend, counsellor or coach and explore the insights that emerge for you.[7]

An important part of this process is to suspend judgement, connect with curiosity and be committed to growth and moving forward. These attributes helped Lara to look honestly at her situation and her role within it, and to take action.

PROCESS

Lara mapped out a description of 'these people': the type of people Lara termed as draining. She described how she met them; the circumstances surrounding their meeting; and what attracted her to them.

She sketched out the process of how the friendships developed. This enabled her to see a pattern, which helped her to identify potentially

---

[7] Refer to the support group list at the end of this book.

similar situations in the future and to act earlier to extract herself before the situations became more difficult.

She listed what she got from the friendships; what the payback was for her. She looked at both the positive and less positive aspects.

This process of discovery resulted in Lara growing as a person; understanding more about who she was; and how she showed up in the world. She also discovered what was important for her; what she held as important; and how this was, at times, expressed in an unhealthy way.

It enabled her to take action. She put firm boundaries in place to keep friendships/professional acquaintances separate by realising that she often befriended good clients and that impacted the professional relationship. Lara commented that she often lost good clients and gained some bad friends.

Lara volunteered as a mentor in a program that helped young female entrepreneurs. This allowed her to give back; contribute her expertise; and support others in their journey, in a healthy and structured way.

Lara invested in an accredited mentor training program to help her keep the mentoring relationships on a professional level. This provided her with a professional group of mentors/colleagues that she could debrief with when she found herself in potentially difficult situations. It also filled a gap in her circle: she realised that she often struggled to talk in detail to her friends about her work challenges and success. This new group of friends filled this gap and she continues to have strong friendships and professional relationships with her mentoring colleagues.

Below are some questions designed to stimulate further thinking and reflection.

1. What drains you?
2. What are your three biggest challenges?
3. Make a list of all the things that you are tolerating in your life. (We put up with, accept, take on. We are dragged down by situations, problems, and others' and our own behaviour. You are tolerating more than you think: so what are you tolerating?)
4. When do you give your power away?
5. What makes you happy?
6. When are you able to laugh at yourself?
7. What is your passion in life? What makes you happiest/most fulfilled?
8. For what gift would you be encouraged to orientate your life around?
9. If time and resources were not a concern: describe the things you long to do?
10. How willing are you to make substantial changes?
11. Think about two people—known to you—who really inspire you: what is it about them that inspires you?
12. Now look forward 20 years. You are attending a function where someone is giving a speech about *you*: What would you want them to say? What do you contribute that is unique?

Notes:

One of the basic rules of the universe is that nothing is perfect. Perfection simply doesn't exist ...Without imperfection, neither you nor I would exist.

Stephen Hawking

CH.9 PERFECTION: LIFE'S GREATEST CON

Perfection is an illusion that we created; it's not real; it's unachievable and simply doesn't exist. In *A Brief History of Time,* Stephen Hawking (1998) says, 'The universe doesn't allow perfection'. I feel that Mr Hawking is a credible source on these matters.

It feels kind of crazy to spend your life striving for something that simply doesn't exist; that is unattainable; and rains negative emotion upon us. How hysterical is the human condition? We all fall prey to illusions about what will be and what is.

Perfection is shiny. It makes all sorts of promises—a bit like living constantly with a sole focus of dreaming of a better future and neglecting the reality of your life and situation. It provides us with wonderful excuses for not doing that thing we want because it is new, or because it stretches us far beyond our comfort zone.

CASE STUDY: ANNA

My friend Anna would constantly call me to complain about her life. The story was the same each time: she was frustrated with her lack of material wealth, her inability to get her entrepreneurial ideas off the ground and the intense frustration when a failure to achieve something had resulted in someone else launching something similar in the market place.

The script varied but the conversation remained the same. It usually went like this, 'It's just not fair. I had that idea. Mine was better. What's wrong with me? I am so tired of being broke. It's OK for you, you can go on holidays'.

Anna was broke (financially) and this was the cause of her distress. She was living from one week to the next and in her words she was, 'Just over it. I'm sick of being poor and not being able to do the things I want'. Anna's problem wasn't the lifestyle she had chosen, it was the fact that she still made choices that brought her dissatisfaction and misery.

Anna is highly intelligent and entrepreneurial. She has fabulous ideas, spends hours dreaming, planning and designing. But she never implemented any of them.

She meditates and writes affirmations, and sticks them all around her house. She is in tune with that side of herself. Like many people (myself included) she finds it valuable to have visible meaningful quotes and pictures that will inspire her.

Our conversations shifted when she called, distraught, 'I am such a failure'. We talked again about her ideas and looked at her resistance at **getting into action** and **implementing something**. The conversation looped back to perfection. Anna fiercely held onto perfection and was very reluctant to loosen her grip on it.

I pointed out that we had been having this same conversation for years. She had clearly chosen to live this way and it was time to either accept the lifestyle that it brings or to change it. What I couldn't do was continue to have the same conversation with her.

Understandably she was angry at this observation.

When I asked her why she never actions any of her ideas, her answer was always, 'It's just not quite right yet'.

Anna is a self-confessed perfectionist. She wears her perfection with pride and it had become an important part of her identity. From an early age, Anna never felt satisfied with her achievements—they were never good enough and she felt pressure to do it again. 'I remember crying most of the school holidays, one year, when I got an A- for English. I expected an A+.' She also shared that she received an award at senior school and was too terrified about the pressure of having to do the same again the following year to be able to enjoy the awards presentation. Anna lived with an enormous amount of self-imposed pressure—a tough way to exist.

This type of pressure is rampant in our society. When we aren't putting pressure on ourselves, others step in. In her TEDx talk, *Your elusive creative genius* (2009), Elizabeth Gilbert shares that one of the results of her international best-selling book *Eat Pray Love* (2006) was that people began to treat her as if she were doomed, *'Seriously ... doomed, doomed!'*

People would ask her:

> Aren't you afraid you're never going to be able to top that? Aren't you afraid you're going to keep writing for your whole life and you're never again going to create a book that anybody in the world cares about at all, ever again?

This wasn't new for Gilbert. She reminisced to a time when she was a teenager and first started telling people that she wanted to be a writer. She was met with the same fear-based reaction with people saying:

Aren't you afraid you're never going to have any success? Aren't you afraid the humiliation of rejection will kill you? Aren't you afraid that you're going to work your whole life at this craft and nothing's ever going to come of it and you're going to die on a scrap heap of broken dreams with your mouth filled with bitter ash of failure?

This is an enormous amount of pressure and self-doubt to manage. When we get a handle on our own negative self-talk, it streams in from elsewhere. The term 'one-hit wonder' needs to be laid to rest.

Anna's focus, like a lot of perfection addicts, was on where she felt she failed; on what she felt was missing; and on fear. Anna, like many people, was battling her own fears, and they were made larger by the fear of others projecting towards her. This is kryptonite to the perfectionist.

Anna shared a fabulous story she had written; it has never seen the light of day because, 'it isn't quite finished yet'. A lot of Anna's projects never saw the light of day because, for her, they were not quite finished. The world was missing out on the gift of an amazing person who is deeply intelligent, funny and talented.

Anna viewed perfection as a strength, something to strive for and by which to live. I invited her to view perfection as a trait, neither good nor bad, strong nor weak. From this place of objectivity, I asked her to make a list of all the things *being a perfectionist* gave her—she wrote a long list.

Here are the main items Anna circled as the ones that stood out most for her:

1. drive – pursuit of excellence
2. stretch and depth
3. attention to detail
4. guilt
5. procrastination
6. critical of self and others.

Through this exercise, Anna was able to see the benefits and limitations of perfectionism, and was then able to take a more balanced stance. She looked at her life and her projects, and applied some conscious thinking around using her tendency for perfection to her advantage and letting go where it was derailing her.

For example, she kept her meditation—her spiritual practice—which was an important part of who Anna was; she didn't want to lose this as it provided her many gifts and supported her wellbeing.

However, on its own, this approach wasn't delivering for Anna. Continuing to solely focus on this approach, Anna realised she would be meditating on the pavement while her furniture and house were being repossessed.

Rather than replacing or deleting aspects of how she operated, we focused on adding the missing pieces—those which Anna needed in order to achieve the life she wanted.

She needed to add some action. She needed tangible goals, linked to her expectations and clear accountability for implementing these as well as committing to implementing projects before they were 100% perfect—a state she recognised was unachievable.

Anna wanted every project to be perfect: 100% ready. We negotiated. My opening bid was 60%. Anna was horrified. She came straight back with 90%. After some tough negotiating Anna agreed that she would adhere to 80%. The next step was to get clarity on what 80% looked like, to set tangible benchmarks, and see how she would measure this and set up a structure surrounding accountability.

In Chapter 8, I spoke about two paths in life: misery or joy. Chasing perfection in every aspect of your life is certainly a fast track option to misery. The more of a perfectionist you are the less satisfied you are.

Perfection is like a pair of glasses: it's just a lens from which we choose to view the world

This lens begins early in a young girl's life. She receives messages about being good, which becomes a currency, something attached to her sense of self and self-esteem. She is often highly praised for her achievements, when what she also needs is praise for her grit, her determination, her creativity, her resilience and her tenacity.

Brené Brown PhD, a research professor and the author of the #1 New York Times best-selling book *The Gifts of Imperfection* (2010), spoke about shame and its link to perfectionism in her TEDx talk, *The power of vulnerability* (2010), which had over 15 million views. If you haven't seen this talk, please google it now (details at the back of this book). It is very insightful and inspirational. Her comment about **women and shame** resonates strongly, 'For women, shame is to do it all, do it perfectly and never let them see you sweat'. She also talked about the conflicting, unattainable messages women have about who they think they are supposed to be. She compares this to a strait jacket.

We are fed so many images and beliefs about whom we are supposed to be and about what we are supposed to be able to handle, that it would make the most hardened superhero crumple. It's worth remembering that superheroes are fictional as are a lot of the promises made by perfection.

Psychologists and scientists debate what is viewed as positive perfectionism and detrimental perfectionism. This resonated for Anna. She could see aspects of her attachment to perfectionism that proved valuable and where they helped her excel in her expectations. However, these examples sat in the shadows of what she termed the, 'big bad perfection monster that ate all my goals'.

Giving yourself space to make mistakes and fail without attaching this to who you are is a great personal gift. Remember, some of life's greatest inventions came from mistakes.

I feel it's important to note that perfectionism, and all its glory and terror, isn't a gender-based issue. It's a human issue and impacts both men and women.

One isn't necessarily born with courage, but one is born with potential. Without courage, we cannot practice any other virtue with consistency. We can't be kind, true, merciful, generous, or honest.

Maya Angelou

No one can make you feel inferior without your consent.

Eleanor Roosevelt

Don't ask yourself what the world needs, ask yourself what makes you come alive. And then go and do that. Because what the world needs is people who have come alive.

Howard Washington Thurman

CH.10 TAKE A STAND FOR YOU

I often pose the following question to clients when they are working through a situation and are being hard on themselves: What would you say to your best friend if they were in the same situation? Or if they have a daughter: what would you advise your daughter if she came to you with the same scenario?

We are loyal and fierce about our best friends, our daughters, our sisters, our nieces and others whom we love and care about. Take some of this fierceness and loyalty and give it to yourself, as the L'Oréal ad says, 'You're worth it'. Bring forward the courage you already possess.

Think back to a time when you stood up for something you believed in; when you connected deeply with a strong *no not that* and stood firm; when no matter what obstacles were in your way or how fearful you were, you moved forward with purpose and focus—you were aligned with your values, your beliefs and your mission.

Do you remember that time?

Yes, you were most likely fearful but almost certainly drew upon courage and reserves of inner strength. This courage and strength is still within you; it can get squashed or exhausted from having to compete with negativity you collected throughout your life. The best line of defence for this is to starve the negativity of thought and, therefore, of life. Hear the voice and move on.

Think about the negative messages you have collected over the years.

Now take a moment and jot them down in the table provided.

Message	Voice/Source	Age

Whose voice do you hear when you read back over the list?

— the saboteur

— a parent

— a critic

— someone else?

This isn't an invitation to attribute blame to others or to beat yourself up. It's about recognising *the voice*, hearing the message and choosing whether you are still willing to live as if it were true. All these voices belong to you.

At some point you made the choice to hold this voice's message as true. Suspend any judgement and please hold off from using this discovery to beat yourself up. Get curious. Ask yourself: What messages have I collected over the years? How do these messages serve me? How do they not serve me?

We hear messages throughout our lives and depending on our age, circumstances and environment, we allocated meaning to these words. My youngest daughter told me recently how upset she was about something I said to her a few months ago. She had taken the words, and made them mean something to her, which didn't reflect the situation or intent. I am delighted that I had the opportunity to have a conversation with her so that it didn't grow into something bigger and contribute to feelings of hurt and anger.

There are times in our lives when we are subjected to hurtful words and situations, we can't change these events; however, we can change how we feel about them and what we make these events mean to us today. I appreciate that depending on what you may be facing, that this can be challenging. I also know how rewarding it is—a personal, true gift to help move you forward, and to choose consciously whether to continue to live your life weighed down by these events.

There is more at play here than just words. Add tone of voice, facial expressions and how we are feeling at the time and you have a very wide playing field. When others give us information, we choose its meaning: we gather evidence to support it or gather evidence to prove it's not true. This takes a lot of energy even when gathering of evidence becomes a way of being; when we are no longer conscious of doing it. This can wreak havoc on our lives, denting our self-esteem and confidence, especially if we are collecting evidence that supports a negative view of ourselves. Of course, the opposite can be true when we collect evidence to support our strengths, our determination and our drive.

If a feeling is triggered by a past incident, an angry word or by someone deliberately wanting to undermine and hurt you, look at where it falls within your timeline. Is it so far back that you can call it history? History is studied and overcome. It has happened. We are in control now of whether we continue to repeat this history.

It can be valuable to look at why you are still holding these feelings of upset, resentment and possibly fear. I believe that it's more important to let them go. Find forgiveness and set yourself free from the limitations brought by holding on to the negative emotions of anger and hurt.

When Caroline did the following exercise she was surprised to find that she also noted some positive messages. At first this confused her.

Message	Voice/Source	Age
You are amazing	Mother	For as long as I can remember

As she explored this, she noticed a pattern of behaviour resulting from often feeling 'not amazing enough'. She became very self-critical in these circumstances. If she didn't achieve a goal, she would feel 'less than amazing'. Caroline realised that she would constantly beat herself up for feeling like a failure. She was doing her best to live up to being amazing all the time. A tough ideal by which to live. If she didn't achieve amazing results, or if she didn't feel amazing, she would make that mean she was a failure and that she would be a disappointment to her parents. This insight helped her to adjust her self-talk and the messages she was giving herself.

There is significant research into the impact of overpraising children and what impact this has. Carol Dweck (2007), is a Stanford Study Professor and author of *Mindset*. In a 2013 interview with Stanford News, Dweck says that telling children, '"You're great, you're amazing," [is] not helpful. Because later on, when [children] don't get it right or don't do it perfectly, they'll think they aren't so great or amazing'.

If this exercise has ignited a deeper curiosity or triggered a past issue that causes you discomfort, sadness or is upsetting, please talk to a trusted friend or consider having a session with a counsellor to help you develop a deeper understanding of the impact this has had and is having on you. This investment will help you move forward.[8]

---

[8] Please refer to the support group list at the back of this book.

There is only one of you in all time, this expression is unique. And if you block it, it will never exist through any other medium and it will be lost.

Martha Graham

CH.11 BE YOUR BEST SELF

Our deepest fear is not that we are inadequate. Our deepest fear is that we are powerful beyond measure. It is our light, not our darkness that most frightens us. We ask ourselves, 'Who am I to be brilliant, gorgeous, talented, and fabulous?' Actually, who are you not to be?

You are a child of God. Your playing small does not serve the world. There is nothing enlightened about shrinking so that other people won't feel insecure around you. We are all meant to shine, as children do. We were born to make manifest the glory of God that is within us. It's not just in some of us; it's in everyone.

And as we let our own light shine, we unconsciously give other people permission to do the same. As we are liberated from our own fear, our presence automatically liberates others.
Marianne Williamson (1996)

BE THE BEST VERSION OF YOU

There is something unique and special about you, something that only you bring to the world. Be the best version of you rather than a paler copy of someone else.

Others have already connected with this in you. They see you. Honour yourself and them by doing the same. Dare to see the uniqueness, the magnificence in you.

In her book *A Return to Love*, Marianne Williamson (1996) says that when we let our own light shine, we give others permission to do the same. It's a wonderful gift to give back to the world. When we dull our own light, we extinguish our brilliance. We fast track towards unhappiness, discontent and misery attracting and picking up others who do the same. This normalises our mindset and the outcomes and we collude with others creating a belief while collecting evidence that this is what life is like—not a good club of which to be a part; it may be time to ditch your membership.

Get conscious about how you are showing up for yourself and for others and the impact this has on you, others and the world in which you live.

We are conditioned to see beauty in others and not in ourselves. It can feel uncomfortable to see our own brilliance, to acknowledge it and to let it shine. I'm not talking about creating a shrine in honour of you and broadcasting this to the world, I'm suggesting that you take time to *really* look at who you are, acknowledge the brilliance others see in you and dare to see the same. The first part of any journey of discovery begins with awareness of self, of who you are and what you bring to the world.

How can you continue to develop this part of you and to let it show up more fully in your life?

As you read this, notice if you are connecting with your uniqueness, denying it or searching for it. How do you connect with what's unique about you?

Write down the first thing that pops into your head right now. Scribble it in this box.

The Strengths Exercise

One of the exercises I often give participants in career programs is to email 20 people and ask them to email you your strengths. Try it. It's a great way to connect with the strengths that others see in you, so you can also see them.

This exercise ignites exploration and conversation. It helps you see your strengths, apply them and gives you means to continue to develop them. It's a stepping stone to access what's unique about you.

This request often receives a mixture of responses from participants and a certain amount of squirming. It can feel a bit uncomfortable. Some point blank refuse, others negotiate and decide that they can maybe email 5–10 people, and some dive right in to the challenge. I challenge people to hear the reasons and excuses of why they cannot enter fully into this challenge.

Some reasons include:

1. People will think it's weird.
2. What if no one emails me back?
3. It feels a bit self-important/self-indulgent.

I assure them that in all the years I have given this challenge, no one has come back to me and said that people have responded in a negative way; no one has been issued any restraining orders nor received a 'get lost, you weirdo' response. To their surprise, the people to whom they reached out have been happy to respond and will often ask if they could also email them their strengths in return.

Remember, you are going to ask people that you know and who know you. Mix it up a bit. To get a balance you might include some friends or work colleagues.

And here's what usually happens: you receive some emails back that will delight and sometimes surprise you. People will connect with your strengths and what you bring.

Be prepared that not everyone will respond. Please don't personalise this. Not everyone is on top of their emails. Send the email and detach from who hasn't responded and focus on the responses you have received.

Building on your strengths is a great way to begin the journey into connecting with what makes you unique.

Strengths Exploration Exercise

Email a minimum of 20 people. I have added some suggested wording to help you but you can adapt and change the wording as you see fit.

> I have been given a challenge to email those whose opinion I value and trust and to ask them to email me my strengths as they see them. I would be grateful if you could do this by (insert date, it always helps to have a deadline).

Please note that you are not putting a number on this, or asking for your top strengths. Keep it wide open to give space for their response. And remember, when you receive your emails be sure to thank them.

Once you have gathered the information, ask yourself the following questions:

1. What stands out for you?
2. Which strengths resonate with you? (You expected these.)
3. What surprised you? (You may not have expected these.)
4. Of what are you most proud?
5. What will you do with this information?
6. How can you incorporate this information into your personal and professional life by finding ways and opportunities to continue to develop your strengths?

SURVEY OF CHARACTER

Take the VIA Survey. At time of writing this book, the basic strengths survey was a free exercise. Explore the VIA Institute on Character website. They provide great articles about discovering and building on your strengths.

1. Buddy up. Gather some friends, colleagues and people with whom you love to hang out. This is a great exercise for your success group to do together. Discuss the questions in point 2.
2. Put your strengths on a board where you can see them every day.
3. Collate the emails and keep them somewhere where you can view them when needed. There may be times when you are feeling less confident or a little down. Reading these emails is a fabulous tonic for lifting your spirits and mood.

When you are taking on new challenges, you can connect with the strengths you have to help you to achieve your goals. When you take on new roles or are making a career decision, ask yourself if this role or project utilises your strengths. The more of your strengths that you are able to bring to what you do, the more opportunity there is to continue to develop them, and according to the founders of positive psychology, the higher the level of fulfilment.

As the gift that keeps on giving, I encourage you to do this exercise as it will help you to:

— understand yourself better
— connect with your strengths and how others see you
— appreciate your uniqueness.

Enjoy.

In the long run, we shape our lives, and we shape ourselves. The process never ends until we die. And the choices we make are ultimately our own responsibility.

Eleanor Roosevelt

CH.12 CHANGE THE SENTENCE

17 years ago, my good friend Tracy Fitzpatrick shared an experience and insight that has stayed with me over the years. It created a powerful, personal impact; one which was especially useful when I made the overwhelming decision to sell my share of The Company and return to Australia, where I had no professional connections.

The Sentence I was running was, *I am overwhelmed and don't know what I am going to do.* This sentence created panic; chipped away at my self-esteem—I felt stuck and powerless. The new sentence was, *I am doing what is right for me. I feel this at the very core of who I am.*

My sentence may not mean anything to anyone else; however, it was and remains incredibly meaningful to me. It helped me create a new perspective from which to rebuild my life and move forward.

It always amazes me how some very simple changes in our outlook and approach can have such a profound impact on our lives.

We create meaning out of our experiences and from what others say and do. Once that meaning is accepted, we create our reality. Sometimes this is helpful and sometimes it is not.

Tracy, thank you for an incredibly valuable gift. It is one I not only still use, but continue to share with my clients, my friends and my daughters.

I asked Tracy to share her experience and technique of *Change the Sentence* so that you can also benefit from this powerful process.

Following is Tracy's gift, in her own words ...

Dear Pollyanna

Thank you for asking me to tell my story. It takes me back 30 years, so I hope I remember to tell it well enough and as you remember it.

(So much has happened since the event that ignited Change the Sentence including loss of memory, I'm sure. The emotional pain fades but was still impacting me when I told you this story.)

So here goes ...

In 1985 my father was dying of cancer. I remember towards the end he had been moved to a private room. One evening my mother, two brothers and I went to visit him. I had cut my hair some weeks previous (for my 21st) and I knew my father had not been keen on the style. Anyway, this one evening my mother was sitting next to my father's bedside and my two brothers and I were standing at the window. My father spoke to both my brothers and to this day I remember my father turning to my mother and saying, 'Make sure Tracy is OK'. As my mother pointed to where I was standing indicating to him I was there he looked through me and repeated a few times to her, 'Make sure Tracy is OK'.

My father passed away a few days later.

I was devastated, as you can imagine. Grief is a strange feeling, and the impact is different each time you lose someone. However, I had become fixated that my father not recognising me but recognising my brothers had some significance to how he felt about me.

It was over the next few years, when I was travelling, that I met some people who really explored the power of words and stories. My father was a fanatic about using the right word, so instantly, anything like that sparked my curiosity. I remember a very good Australian friend of mine, Kevin, telling me how he didn't let people look after his children as he didn't believe they took the time to explain things to them correctly. As an example he told me he caught a relative telling his eldest not to play on the road as it was dangerous. He grabbed a ball and took his eldest daughter, Georgia, on to the road and played ball. He then explained the road is made of tarmac and isn't dangerous; however, cars come along and might injure you so he'd rather she played in the park. The more I spoke with Kevin, the more I learnt from him about words and stories. He was an extraordinary man who changed my life, and I was privileged to be asked to his 3rd child's birthing party.

The demon of that night in hospital when my father did not recognise me still hung over me. I felt and accepted it would be with me forever, as I couldn't shake it. With everything I had learned from Kevin, I began to wonder, *what if I changed the words and the story for that one night*. In order to do this I had to look at the picture and change the story to keep it real. All I needed to do to change the story was take the emotion and drama out of it and keep it real. This changed my sentence.

When I looked at the picture, the facts were that on the night my father didn't recognise me, he was on morphine and I had changed my hair style. These were the facts. There could have been a number of reasons he didn't recognise me, none of which were the emotional, dramatic ones I had concocted, that's for sure.

The relief was instant, and I've never looked back since.

I then thought about this and it made sense: how often we have things mean something (usually emotional or with drama) and make them the truth. This is when I thought of Change the Sentence, and this is when my life started to become better.

By changing the sentence you can keep it real. If you take the emotion and drama out of the situation, it puts things into perspective and possibly brings it closer to the truth.

I hope I have captured my story today, as I told it to you many years ago.

All the very best

Tracy

TRACY'S PROCESS FOR CHANGING THE SENTENCE IS:

1. VISUALISE (the picture)

Visualise the picture of when the event happened or when something was said.

2. REALITY (no emotion/drama)

Ask yourself: what is the reality of the event, without the emotion and drama?

3. CHANGE (YOUR SENTENCE)

Change the sentence to keep it real and in perspective.

Tracy's process for changing the sentence is a way to get conscious and to re-examine what we have chosen to hold as true and to change this if it is causing us distress or upset, or delivering results with which we are less than happy.

The negative impact of creating our lives from a place of hurt and anger is well documented with more evidence based research emerging to support this being published.

Deepak Chopra (2014) says, 'It's not easy to deal with painful emotions head-on. But it's a key to good health and well-being physically, mentally and spiritually. If we don't deal with pain when it occurs, it will resurface as compounded *emotional toxicity* later on – showing up as insomnia, hostility and anger or fear and anxiety.'

When we identify and let go of thoughts and beliefs that are keeping us stuck, angry and hurt, our lives improve. As in Tracy's situation, years of stored anger and hurt began to melt away. Her response to other situations, which triggered these feelings also changed. By changing her sentence she also changed her path and future.

What sentences are you carrying that cause you hurt, anger and pain?

_____

_____

_____

_____

_____

Is it time to change these sentences? ☐ YES   ☐ NO

What are the new sentences?

_____

_____

_____

_____

_____

We cannot live better than in seeking to become better.

Socrates

CH.13 SUCCESS AND HOW YOU FEEL

Years ago, my good friend Natarsha shared something with me that just made so much sense. It sounded so incredibly easy and impacted significantly on how she felt.

Natarsha decided to remove everything in her wardrobe that made her feel average and only kept what she felt fabulous wearing. She decided to wear her best clothes every day. I thought this was brilliant. We often postpone feeling good and whilst clothes are external there is no doubt that wearing clothes that make you feel fabulous has a positive impact on how you feel. It can transform negative feelings, enhance mood, impact how we feel about ourselves and how we influence others.

The conversation with Natarsha led me to think about the belief I carried from my childhood about *saving your best dress for special occasions*. The reality of living this belief is that our best remains in the wardrobe gathering dust.

This isn't about wearing the latest fashion or spending a fortune on a new wardrobe. It is about employing simple strategies that help us feel confident and fabulous every day, and reaping the benefits of the great feeling this bestows upon us. Try it.

Professor Karen Pine conducted research on how a person's attire affects confidence. She found students were more assured when wearing a Superman t-shirt and women performed worse in a maths test when donning a swimsuit. That makes sense to me.

Intrinsically we know this. We forget about the valuable payback for taking time to invest in the small things that make us feel great—the low hanging fruit of self-esteem, confidence and feeling good.

This and other research appears in her book *Mind What You Wear: The Psychology of Fashion (2014)*. In an interview with the Daily Mail Australia, she concludes that the right or wrong clothes can affect your attitude.

Dr Alastair Tomb is the lead researcher of a group of psychologists from Queensland University who conducted research into the psychology of mood and clothes, and how we use clothes to improve mood or to mask emotion. He says,

> We demand many things from clothing. Quite a few people talked about using clothes to change their mood. If they get up and aren't feeling great, they would put on something that would brighten them up.
>
> On other occasions they use clothes to mask their emotions. It didn't brighten their mood, but it would give them the appearance of being bright and airy, even if that is not how they actually feel.

Doing a wardrobe edit and getting rid of everything in which you feel less that wonderful, may be a good investment of a few hours of your time.

It's difficult to stand out, to shine and to influence when coming from a foundation of doubt.

Make celebrating your achievements a regular part of your life. Like sunlight, celebration nourishes our growth and our soul. It can serve to keep us motivated and focused on our path; it also serves to remind us of the things that we have achieved and gives some space for this to take centre stage for a while.

Pollyanna Lenkic

CH. 14 MAKE SPACE FOR CELEBRATION

A common theme among women with whom I have worked and interviewed is a reluctance to celebrate their own achievements and to acknowledge that their role contributed to or was a direct result of an achievement, either personal or professional. Despite amazing achievements, language is still peppered with *I was lucky, I was in the right place at the right time*, and *I'm not sure I deserve this*. This is often to an extent beyond being humble and is detrimental to both the woman running the dialogue—internally and externally—and to her impact at home, at work and in the world. I want the best for you and the world needs the best of you. For you to bring your best at home, at work and into the world and to make a difference, you must first dare to see it within yourself.

It's difficult to stand out, to shine and to influence when coming from a foundation of doubt.

Each time you say, *I was lucky and I was in the right place at the right time, or it wasn't really me, I had a great team behind me* and attribute this as the sole reason for your success: you miss out on so much of you, your hard work and the gift of your experience that can be shared for others to model, strive toward and benefit from. You miss out on acknowledgment of your achievements—both internally and externally—and you miss out on the confidence that builds when you *own* your achievements and success.

Yes, often the stars align. Success is built from many factors, and timing and opportunity play a part. The piece that is often overlooked and then negated is the years of hard work, study, grit and determination that got you there.

When I reflect on my past conversations about how lucky I was to have been given the opportunity to build a company, I left out that I also worked for that opportunity. I hit a lot of 5 am starts, and I worked late throughout the week and into weekends. I gave it all I had. I pushed through uncertainty and, at times, crippling fear of failure to achieve my goals and provide the best service I could for my clients.

Was I lucky? Yes, absolutely. I felt and do still feel incredibly fortunate to have had that opportunity; however, that sentence now has a different energy for me. Feeling lucky for the opportunity to build SQ comes from a place of gratitude for the opportunity itself, and the experience, knowledge and the future it provided.

How many times have you read an 'overnight success' article? What these articles often leave out is the 10+ years of preparation, hard work, sweat and tears that attributed to the success. The years of gathering knowledge and the hours of hard work developing skills and competence is often what led to the success. Malcolm Gladwell (2011) defines this concept in his book *Outliers: The Story of Success* referencing the **10,000-hour rule** (based on research by Anders Ericsson), stating that the key to success is a matter of practicing a specific task for a total of around 10,000 hours.

So does this mean that if we dedicate 10,000 hours to any task or goal, we will become superstars? If we take it literally, I would think not—no matter how much time I dedicate to becoming a gymnastics champion, this goal may be beyond me.

However, combining what you love with what you are good at (your strengths) and in what you invest (applying the 10,000-hour rule) will get you far on your journey to achieving your goal and success. It will also provide the gift of showing you what you don't already know about yourself, your abilities and what's available to you. In the same way that we are educating our children for jobs that don't yet exist, by focusing on developing ourselves personally, professionally and spiritually we are preparing ourselves for a future of which we are not yet aware and the opportunities and fulfilments that will be available. This requires hard work and investment in yourself, in your mind set, your skillset and your communication techniques.

We must take action for anything to happen. It's not something you can *try*, it's something that you have actually to do.

Exercise

Put an object in front of you, for example, a pen, and try to pick it up.

When I ask people to do this they lean forward and pick up the pen. I ask them to put it down and say, 'No, you actually picked it up, just *try* to pick it up'.

Eventually, after some laughter, I make my point: the only way to pick up the pen is by action, reaching forward with your hand and picking it up.

We don't ever achieve anything by trying. We achieve by doing, by getting into action.

So now, by combining getting into action with focusing on *what you love*, *what you are good at*, and in *what you choose to invest*, you will be provided the **expertise** to excel, and the **fulfilment** and **passion** to keep you motivated and on track and moving towards your **purpose**.

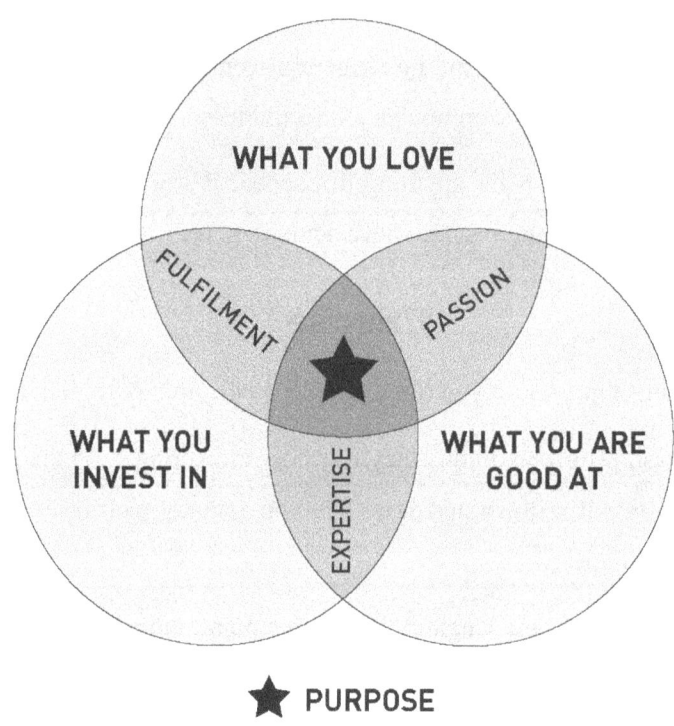

What's your 10,000 hours of expertise? Or the expertise you are working towards? As well as looking at your professional life, I invite you to look back further. In what area have you developed expertise? How has this shaped your life? How has this contributed to who you are, what you do and where you may be headed?

Success, like life, isn't one dimensional: it is a kaleidoscope of colour and variation. It's time to give colour and prominence to the areas in your kaleidoscope; those that represent effort, stamina, learning, hard work and the courage it took to create your success. Bring this into your communication with both yourself and others.

What is your expertise? What gift and skill do you bring?

CASE STUDY: CLARA

Clara is a talented woman who has achieved remarkable success and is at the top of her field. Here is her story:

When I first took on this role I began experiencing recurring nightmares. The dream always started with me sitting at my desk in my open plan office. Suddenly, all the lights would go out. I felt an intense fear creep into me while sitting there in the dark. Then I would hear a loud shout of *HEY YOU THERE*. And a spotlight would illuminate me. I felt panicked and screamed, *Oh no, they have found out*. Then the scene would switch to me looking at myself from above and I would get smaller and smaller until I was a speck on the ground. I woke up feeling anxious and terrified thinking, *Is today the day they discover I am a fraud?* This went on for months, and only started to settle down after I signed my permanent contract with the company and got some coaching support.

I still get anxious about new roles; however, not as bad as I used to.

Clara is not alone. *Impostor syndrome* is well researched and documented and often attributed as being specific to women. Let's clarify Impostor Syndrome.

In 1978, Dr Pauline Rose Clance and Suzanne Imes from Georgia State University published a paper *The Impostor Phenomenon in High Achieving Women: Dynamics and Therapeutic Intervention.*

The term *Impostor Phenomenon* was used to describe a psychological phenomenon where a person was unable to recognise their accomplishment regardless of any evidence of their achievements and competence. People experiencing Impostor Syndrome would remain firmly convinced they didn't deserve their success, that they were frauds and would be discovered as such.

'Proof of success is dismissed as luck, timing, or as a result of deceiving others into thinking they are more **intelligent** and competent than they believe themselves to be.'[9]

Over a 5-year period, Imes and Clance worked with more than 150 highly-successful women who had achieved high levels of academic and professional success and were highly respected by their peers and students. They defined Impostor Phenomenon as, 'An internal experience of intellectual phonies, which appears to be particularly prevalent and intense among a select sample of high achieving women'.

Imes and Clance noted that

> ... despite their earned degrees, scholastic honors, high achievement on standardized tests, praise and professional recognition from colleagues and respected authorities, these women do not experience an internal sense of success. They consider themselves to be "impostors." Women who experience the impostor phenomenon maintain a strong belief that they are not intelligent; in fact they are convinced that they have fooled anyone who thinks otherwise.

---

[9] Source: Wikipedia

Imes and Clance's study focused on Impostor Phenomenon and women, and it was believed that this was a condition mainly experienced by women. Further articles and studies also focused on Impostor Phenomenon/Impostor Syndrome being mainly something with which women grappled. However, ongoing research has showed it is also common amongst high achieving men and affects both men and women over a broad range of professions and circumstances.

In an article by Kristen Weir (2013) published by the American Psychological Association, Weir states that, 'The impostor phenomenon and perfectionism often go hand in hand. So-called impostors think every task they tackle has to be done perfectly, and they rarely ask for help'.

Impostor Syndrome is a human condition not a gender condition. Both men and women can get trapped in the spiral of consequences that result from feeling like an impostor.

Women are courageous. They are ready to speak up and be vulnerable; the world benefits from this. Anyone who has seen Brené Brown's TEDx talk or read her books and research would be hard pressed to dismiss the gift and power that comes with thoughtful vulnerability.

Are we owning Impostor Syndrome? Are we owning it as a women-only issue, thus allowing us to limit our potential, success and happiness?

We need to change the landscape of what we are owning as women—that which doesn't belong uniquely to us.

We can help by clearly communicating that Impostor Syndrome is not a women's issue; it's a business and global issue. It's a condition that affects both men and women and results in loss of opportunity for individuals, organisations and the world.

Both women and men can benefit from having these conversations; by normalising it and removing isolation, doubt and shame.

What is unique to women according to Katty Kay and Claire Shipman, authors of the 2014 paper *The Confidence Gap* is the impact when women doubt themselves. They discuss that confidence matters as much as competence when it comes to success and that women are less self-assured than men and allow this doubt to limit their potential:

'Do men doubt themselves sometimes? Of course. But they don't let their doubts stop them as often as women do.'

Confidence, like comfort zones, require dedicated focus and support to get you through and move forward. Treat them as neither good nor bad, right nor wrong—they are what they are, and we get to choose their meaning. Confidence is a wonderful thing to have; however, it is not essential to have it in place before stepping up. It's a bit like motivation, the endless wait for motivation, the dedicated strategies to bring on motivation before you actually can do something, needs reversing. Get into action; put your hand up for that new role, new task or new project; start investing in it. Do the work and the motivation and confidence will follow. Waiting for confidence and motivation to come first is a false economy.

Normalising Impostor Syndrome and lack of confidence is good place to start. Understand that if you experience this or have experienced it, it is a shared and common experience. It is the first step to moving from Impostor Syndrome's icy grasp. Just by noticing that you are in it, begins the process of moving forward.

Many well-known people, who have achieved incredible success, talk of feelings of Impostor Syndrome, here are a few:

Dr Valerie Young (2011) author of *The Secret Thoughts of Successful Women* interviewed many high achieving people on Impostor Syndrome including Tina Fey an American actor, comedian, writer and producer. Fey shared her feelings:

'The beauty of the impostor syndrome is you vacillate between extreme egomania and a complete feeling of: "I'm a fraud! Oh God, they're on to me! I'm a fraud!" So you just try to ride the egomania when it comes and enjoy it, and then slide through the idea of fraud.'

In a 60 Minutes interview award-winning actor Jodie Foster talked about her Oscar win for Best Actor for the film The Accused. Here is what she said:

'I thought it was a fluke. [It was] the same way when I walked on the campus at Yale. I thought everybody would find out, and they'd take the Oscar back. They'd come to my house, knocking on the door, "Excuse me, we meant to give that to someone else. That was going to Meryl Streep."'

In an interview with author Susan Pink, Kate Winslet said that fame doesn't give you confidence:

'Sometimes I wake up in the morning before going off to a shoot, and I think, I can't do this. I'm a fraud.'

Michael Uslan, the producer of Batman, shared his occasional bouts of Impostor Syndrome in an interview with the Huffington Post.

'I still have this background feeling that one of the security guards might come and throw me out.'

These responses are common. I have heard similar themes with men and women I have coached over the past 15+ years. I experienced this myself many times over, and have read about it in various research studies and interviews. It's a normal phenomenon. It becomes a problem when it stops you from moving forward and when it dominates your thoughts. In these situations, it's important to seek support through a qualified and experienced counsellor or coach. The choice of whether to work with a coach or counsellor will depend on how deeply the process has impacted you.

We started this section with celebration. It seems a lot can and does get in our way when we embark on celebrating ourselves and our achievements. And, pushing these blocks and excuses aside is a good practice.

Make celebrating your achievements a regular part of your life. Like sunlight, celebration nourishes our growth and our soul. It can serve to keep us motivated and focused on our path; it also serves to remind us of the things that we have achieved and gives some space for this to take centre stage for a while.

I read a beautiful birthday ritual years ago by author Marie-Nathalie Beaudoin (1998) in a book she co-authored *Working with Groups to Enhance Relationships.* She shares a ritual her mother-in-law created. At every birthday party, she invited family members to share something about each year of the honoured child's life as the candles were blown out one by one. When she had her twin girls, she eventually had her two daughters alternate saying something they remembered of each other's life, year-by-year as they blew out the candles one-by-one.

I love this ritual. It is a fabulous framework for creating a tradition of celebration within your family and friendship circles.

We are very good at focusing on what is not working or what we haven't done. We can forget to shine the light on what we have achieved. Remember my friends Amy and Sara, and the conversation we had about success? It's common for women to focus on what they didn't achieve; what went wrong; and where they weren't good enough.

Celebration is often saved for big events and driven by our calendars. Celebrate the small stuff, achievements and wins.

In our society, we have regular calendar dates that remind us to celebrate, to stop and connect with what we are grateful for. In the US, Thanksgiving is a beautiful landmark that provides an opportunity to do this. My invitation is to create your own regular landmark to celebrate the achievements in your life.

Exercise

Gather a group of friends. Place two dates in your calendars (per year) to celebrate together. Ensure a *no cancelling* agreement. Make your celebration day/evening as special as your other landmark celebrations.

Strength does not come from physical capacity; it comes from indomitable will.

Zig Ziglar

CH. 15 JUGGLING:

THE ADDICTION THAT LEADS TO EXHAUSTION

Juggling can be fun, have you ever tried it? You take some colourful balls, usually three, throw them into the air, and maintain the flow, in a circular motion, while keeping all the balls in play.

At a recent community fair, there was a wonderful man dressed as a clown teaching parents and their children the fun art of juggling—we (Sean, my daughters and I) all had a go. There was lots of laughter as we, very unsuccessfully, tried to juggle our brightly coloured balls. We tried various techniques, none of which were successful. The laughs turned into nervous giggles as our balls hit the ground again, and again, *and* again. Frustration started to unravel; however, we kept it under wraps.

It was a busy day for our clown. There was lots of interest in how to juggle. We were determined to get it right; we persevered but became tired. I noticed that other juggling amateurs also became tired. Some walked away, some became irritable, some blamed the balls, some blamed the clown for not showing them how to do it right.

Just as we were about to give up, our friendly clown approached and showed us a technique for successful juggling. We nailed it.

SUCCESS: we were all juggling. There were lots of high fives and competitions on who could juggle the longest, compliments on our juggling techniques and a few smug feelings as we aced it.

But we became more tired and it started to impact the fun. Our necks were sore from looking up, our arms were tired from the continuous movement; therefore, juggling started to lose its shine.

We were still able to juggle, but as our fatigue heightened, we started to drop the balls. I noticed other fallouts. The intensity of primarily focusing on keeping our balls in the air had resulted in a lack of awareness of our environment and of others. We started to bump into each other. Others' concentration was fading too but displayed reactions from humour to anger.

People started to drift off. My youngest daughter and I were still playing, still juggling. We looked up and the clown was packing up, grinning at our antics.

Sometimes the focus of juggling is so intense that you don't realise it's become dark and everyone has gone home.

We (women) are fed a daily diet of how to have it all, how to juggle successfully and with the added expectation that we can and we should.

The reality is that to get through life it takes a certain amount of juggling. We chase the nirvana of a balanced life, while frantically juggling all our balls and expending energy to keep them in the air. Juggling as a way of life, however, like perfection, is failing to deliver on its promise as the answer to having a balanced life.

Despite research showing us that multitasking makes us less efficient and fulfilled, we delude ourselves into thinking that multitasking is our friend and pride ourselves on being able to multitask continually in our professional and personal lives. The reality is this is leading to exhaustion, lack of focus and feelings of failure.

Once we get a few balls in the air and develop a level of competence with keeping these balls moving, it's easy to buy into adding more shiny balls into the mix with the expectation that it's not only possible but required, to keep them in the air.

We chase an ideal of balance that includes a long list of *must haves*. Balance, like juggling, takes effort to maintain.

Pick a pose that requires balance. Now hold that pose. It's completely manageable for a few minutes and in yoga or other practices it is a valuable exercise. Keep practising and your level of expertise and strength grows and it becomes possible to hold the pose for longer the more you practise. Now imagine trying to hold the pose for an hour, two hours, and six hours a day?

There comes a tipping point where juggling and maintaining balance is no longer sustainable. The approach is not serving you and isn't delivering on its perceived rewards.

Regardless of how skilful or committed you are, it *is* impossible not to become fatigued and topple over. The expended energy from trying to regain and retain balance over a long period of time, eventually will lead to frustration, exhaustion and diminishing health.

Personally, I have never subscribed to the mantra of 'having it all'. I do believe in getting very clear about what is important to you and having that, and making decisions about what you want in your life—let's face it, there are many shiny balls out there. This, in itself, can be overwhelming.

A few years ago, I was an advisor to the Board of a wonderful group called The 100. It was a cross-generational networking group set up by a dynamic trio of young professional women, which brought women together to discuss issues faced by women in the workforce. One evening we discussed the issues surrounding maternity leave, and the impact of this on career and choices, both professionally and personally.

One woman stood up to speak—she would have been in her mid-60s—and what she shared had such a profound impact on me that I went home and re-evaluated how I was juggling my life. I thank her for her priceless viewpoint and wisdom.

To the best of my memory, here's what she said:

> I reached a senior level in my career as a CEO of a large multinational company. I still sit on boards. Back when I was CEO, there were very few women CEOs, there were no policies to support women returning to work after having a child and very few people to discuss the challenges that came with this. My husband was an artist and didn't earn a lot of money; therefore, I was responsible for our family's income. I went back to work six weeks after my daughter was born—a decision I have always regretted and felt guilty about. (My daughter assures me that she has never suffered due to my decision to work.)
>
> I decided not to have another child due to the circumstances of my personal and professional life, and I questioned this decision for a long time.

> If I were to offer younger women, here tonight, one piece of advice I would tell you that you have a career span of 40+ years ahead of you. Whether you take six weeks, six months or a year or two of maternity leave, it is a very small amount of time in the greater scheme of your 40+ year career.

Her words held so much wisdom and resonated deeply with me. Following her advice, I decided to reduce the days I was working to three per week. I was exhausted. My youngest daughter, who was 18 months old at the time, wasn't sleeping and I wasn't coping with the schedule I was running. I went back to work too soon after having her. The decision to take a step back was a sound one. It allowed me to regroup, refocus on what was important and replenish. I became clear and focused about the work I was doing, what type of work I would commit to and what work I would not take on.

I chose to reduce my hours, rather than completely take a break, because I believed it was important to invest in continuing to develop skill set, confidence and social/professional interactions. Research shows that a high proportion of women who have experienced death of a spouse or divorce, live in poverty due to struggling to re-enter the workforce at a level required to maintain their previous lifestyle. Leslie Bennetts (2007) tackles this in her book *The Feminine Mistake*. She provides a compelling case for women to think clearly about the longer term impact of opting out of the workforce and becoming financially dependent on a spouse.

By continuing the investment in you and your development, from both a skill set and confidence perspective, you are providing yourself another gift that will keep on giving.

A discussion that often arises, among women with young children, is whether it was worth working when childcare costs absorb most of the money earned. My response is that by continuing to invest in yourself, you will have more options, more confidence and greater choices around your role and salary, when you are ready to dive back into your career.

There are many ways to do this: either engage in the workforce in a way that works for you and your situation or volunteer your time at a charity, school or kindergarten/childcare committee. The social interaction is highly beneficial as is the use of skills and competencies that are required in these roles.

DECISIONS

I believe in getting crystal clear on what it is that's important to you—in the short, medium and long term, and making clear decisions about this. In a recent talk Matt Church, Founder of Thought Leaders Business School, said that to decide is to kill off choice. It comes from the Latin origins dēcīdere, which literally means to cut off. Sometimes life presents so many choices, all very shiny, that in order to decide, it helps to look at the current landscape in which we live, kill off or park some choices and decide what is really important to us and for what we have capacity.

Rather than striving to have it all, get clear about what you want, and what's important to you and have that. This will change depending on your circumstances and where you are in life.

CASE STUDY: ELISSA

Elissa worked for a global organisation that held an annual sales conference in Vietnam. She wanted to go to Vietnam and figured a great way to do this was to convince her company that she was the person to run the conference or to be involved in some capacity; therefore, guaranteeing her place at the conference, doing work she loved and being paid to go to a country she was desperate to visit.

Elissa campaigned for this for a few years. Finally the opportunity arose and she was asked to go. Here is her case:

I called my husband. I was ecstatic about the news. I love lists, so I immediately wrote down all the reasons it was a great idea to go: fabulous opportunity to network and gain profile within the organisation, four days of waking up in a hotel on my own—bliss— and get to go to Vietnam. I had a very long list of pros. My husband was excited for me. He was happy to support my decision and then he asked how I wanted to work out feeding Emma, our second child who was six months old. It wasn't practical to express my breastmilk, and if I were to fulfil my pro list I would have to put Emma on formula. I just couldn't do that. I had a long list of pros but one item on my list of cons.

I realised then and there that I couldn't go. (It wasn't about whether formula or breastfeeding was better.) I decided not to go and felt at peace with that decision.

Elissa shared that for her it was about avoiding a decision that she felt would keep 'repeating on me'. One that regardless of logic and world-health assurances, she knew she would regret the decision to go to Vietnam.

I asked Elissa if she regretted *not* going to Vietnam. She said that while she was initially sad about not going, once she made the decision not to go, she was happy and moved on. She felt that the opportunity or something similar would arise again.

The YES/NO Exercise

15 years ago, when I attended the Co-Active Coaching program by CTI, a course leader shared this very valuable formula. I love it; it's quick and easy and provides me with clarity.

For every YES there is a NO and for every NO there is a YES. Get clear about your YES and NO.

For Elissa, her one NO was more compelling than her many Yes's. What decisions in your life could benefit from looking at YES and NO?

Your beliefs become your thoughts
Your thoughts become your words
Your words become your actions
Your actions become your habits
Your habits become your values
Your values become your destiny.

Mahatma Gandhi

CH. 16 VALUES:

UNDERSTANDING WHAT DRIVES THE CORE OF YOU

Think about the times when your life didn't flow. Those were the times when you felt out of sync. The actions or decisions you made didn't feel quite right, and there was discomfort.

When a situation feels like a struggle, it's often because we are out of alignment with our deepest values.

Think about what you hold as meaningful, what you hold as true for you?

When life is effortless and satisfying, we leap out of bed and experience life from an authentic place, a place where we are behaving and living in alignment with and honouring our values.

Values are a way of measuring what's most important to you in your life. Uncovering and understanding your values helps you to understand yourself, the choices that are important to you and the life of which you will feel proud.

Exploring the topic of success would be missing an important partner if we omitted reflecting on our values. There are different belief systems surrounding values. Some believe that our values change as we grow and transition into different phases of our lives. I believe that our values are intrinsic to who we are, and that they are at the core of us driving our behaviour and choices in life. For me, when I am aligned and making decisions based on my values, life feels authentic; I make better decisions, and I make a lot less mess.

When making decisions consider this simple question: how does this align with my values? This will go a long way in helping you make the decisions that are right for you and with which you can live and be at peace.

Values-based decisions sometimes require you to miss out on an opportunity, or on something that you want, but if something about it feels wrong it is coming from a deep intuitive level. What happened? How did it work out for you?

Engaging in any activity, be it personal or professional, which causes a clash of who you are from a values viewpoint, often delivers hurt, upset and grief. I invite you to think about your values and what you are valuing in your life right now.

The Values Exercise

There are hundreds of exercises to help you to explore your values. I have provided a few for you here. Take some time to connect with the core values that are an intrinsic part of who you are.

Jot down a list of attributes that you feel reflect who you are—the more the merrier. There is no limit. Once you have completed this list, circle the ones that stand out for you. Next, circle the top three—the ones that are most important to you.

Make a list of your past successes. Of which do you feel most proud? Which ones were the most meaningful? What was present that made this so? Write down the words that describe this. You are mining for your values.

Reflect back to the times when life felt out of sync, when decisions that you made caused personal grief and upset. Look deeper than the incident itself and identify the value that was suppressed.

What is most important to you in life? Start writing these down, as quickly as you can, just let your subconscious drive this process, the faster the better. There will be time to review and reflect after you have downloaded your list. Ask yourself: what's important about having this?

Create two lists side-by-side. One is titled *My Values*, the other, *What I am valuing*.

When Joanna did this exercise, she was amazed at how many things she was valuing in her life that weren't serving her. During our coaching sessions, Joanna uncovered that she was placing a huge value on having drama in her life. Drama wasn't a value for Joanna; however, she was valuing it and regularly found ways to have more drama in her world. Once Joanna identified the patterns of behaviour that led to this investment in drama, she was able to let it go.

There is a distinction between our values and what we are valuing. Explore this in your world and decide if what you are valuing is serving you.

My values	What I am valuing

Values: understanding what drives the core of you

Three-part Values Exercise

Here is another exercise; I love this one. Is it from Steve Kormas (The Centre for Management Creativity) with whom I completed NLP training many years ago.

Follow the exercise as written. The key to this is to do it **quickly**.

A. OPENING YOUR MIND

From a relaxed state, I want you to think of the things that you want to have in your life. Make a list of about ten things that you want. Do this quickly. Just allow your pen to do the writing.

1. _____ | _____
2. _____ | _____
3. _____ | _____
4. _____ | _____
5. _____ | _____
6. _____ | _____
7. _____ | _____
8. _____ | _____

9. _____ | _____

10. _____ | _____

As you look at these things, I want you to notice what they have in common. Of course, one of your choices might be to have more money. I want you to focus beyond that; I want you to think about what having money will do for you. A couple of examples would be that money would give you freedom, or status.

In the right-hand column, prioritise your wants from 1–10 in order of most important.

B. GAINS

Look at your *Opening your mind* list. Now write what each of those things would get for you.

1. _____

2. _____

3. _____

4. _____

5. _____

6. _____

7. _____

8. _____

9. _____

10. _____

I invite you to consider these as your true goals.

C. YOUR VALUES

Everyone has a list of values from which he or she live. If you want to manifest something into your life, which violates your values, it's more than likely not going to happen.

List your top ten values. Keep it simple. An example of these values may be health, family, money, honesty, satisfaction, happiness, education, learning, relationships and so on. For this exercise, write them down as you think of them—as quickly as you can.

1. _____

2. _____

3. _____

4. _____

5. _____

6. _____

7. _____

8. _____

9. _____

10. _____ |_____

In the right-hand column, prioritise your values from 1–10 in order of most important.

D. CONFLICTS

Take a moment and examine how the things that you want to draw into your life fit with your top 5 values. Is there conflict between what you want, and your values?

If there is, take a moment to write down the conflict.

_____

_____

_____

_____

_____

_____

_____

_____

Are you willing to adjust your values or adjust what you want to manifest so that they fit together?

This is also a great place in which to *check in* with your beliefs, and about what you want. For example, if you hold the belief that money does not bring you happiness, look at the impact of holding this belief on your enjoyment, and of getting what you want.

By now you will be truly immersed in the exploration of what you value, where the conflicts arise between what you want and what you value and beginning to uncover whether what you are valuing aligns with your values.

I have provided a few extra questions below to keep your mind bubbling on this very important cornerstone of success.

1. I am at my best when …
2. I am deeply inspired when …
3. My most blissful, joyful, positive moments come when …
4. If all else were stripped away, the most important things to me would be …
5. The qualities in people whom I admire are …

Notes:

Your attitude not your aptitude will determine your altitude.

Zig Ziglar

CH.17 COMMUNICATION, POSITIONING AND SUCCESS

CASE STUDY: HANNAH

Hannah was promoted to a senior managerial role that required her to have a weekly meeting with her manager. She was promoted into this role due to her past performance, excellent business knowledge and good leadership skills.

Hannah had a seat at the leadership table because she had the skill, capability and expertise to perform her role and because she had worked hard and earned her place.

She came to our coaching session feeling anxious about her ability to perform this role. As the conversation evolved, Hannah spoke of ownership for issues that didn't belong to her. I could see her confidence drowning as she recounted her most recent catch up with her manager. She was angry, frustrated and was falling into patterns of blame, and the victim mindset.

She felt that her manager had unrealistic expectations of what she could deliver. Given the scenario that Hannah described, her feelings seemed justified. Hannah's contracted hours consisted of a 4-day week. She was 6 months pregnant with her third child; she was exhausted and had been experiencing a difficult pregnancy.

The environment where she worked and the management team that she worked for had little insight or understanding of her personal circumstances. She worked in a male-dominated setting that would have benefited from reviewing its operating model with regards to retaining the talented women within its company.

Hannah was informed that she was required to travel interstate to attend a client meeting. The senior team were to fly in the night before and attend a meeting at 9 pm at the hotel (to give everyone time to arrive) to discuss strategy for the client presentation the next day. This required Hannah to work on her day off, giving her the additional stress of having to arrange childcare for her other two children. With the expectation of a late night looming, Hannah was seething.

Here is an outline of the situation she faced, in her own words.

> I was really excited when I was promoted to the position of general manager of my division after 5 years in a consulting role. The director of the company communicated that he was keen for my learning curve to be steep. He had a tough management style. He was known for this, and his approach with me was tough. At our meetings he would rapidly spill out information followed up with the answers, so all I felt I could do was say:
>
> *OK, I'll take that on board.*
> *OK, that makes sense, thanks for sharing.*
> *OK, thank you. I'll get better at that.*
> *OK, I have lots to learn (nervous laugh).*
>
> I felt his disapproval during our weekly meetings, and I felt like I didn't connect with him or even like him. I would walk away from these meetings feeling like a failure.

Communication, positioning and success

After recounting her experiences Hannah said, 'I know coaching isn't advice but please I'm stuck: what can I do?'

My response was, 'You are going to have to put on your *big girl pants*'.

I got to know Hannah well: she was intelligent with a great sense of humour. After a pause, she dissolved into laughter mixed with a bit of disbelief that she had heard me correctly: did I really say that? Yes, I did.

Sometimes we just have to put on our *big girl pants*, step up and into our expertise that is firmly grounded in our adult selves. We need to do this from a place of self-respect, compassion and honesty.

The first area we looked at was from a perspective of self: What was going on for Hannah? What was important to her? What did she need to own? How was she contributing to the situation? Of what did she need to let go?

Two questions that we explored were:

1. What was causing her to doubt herself and her abilities? We drilled down to understand what was at the heart of this.
2. What were the boundaries that Hannah *blurred* that needed to be put back in place?

We reframed her story from one of inadequacy to take in the reality of the situation. These were the facts:

— Hannah was working above and beyond her contracted hours whilst managing her personal life and a difficult pregnancy.

- She was delivering on her targets. She was backfilling another role (in addition to her own) that had not been filled after another senior team member had left the company.

- Her communication strategy was derailing her and creating doubt with her manager and within herself. She was allowing herself to fall into unhelpful passive aggressive behaviours, which caused conflict, undermined her professionalism and impacted negatively on her position in the company.

We discussed what was out of her control, in her sphere of influence and in her control, by looking at what structures and processes would be helpful to shift her communication style to one that matched her expertise, re-enforced her position as a senior leader in the company, ensured that she only owned the issues that actually belonged to her and re-established firm boundaries around what she was able and willing to commit to and own.

Hannah arrived to our next session a month later feeling a lot more in control, happier and looking a lot more rested. When I asked her what had created the shift she said:

> I changed the language I was using. I removed 'I' unless I owned it and it was a purposeful impact statement.
>
> I talked about what the business needed, from the business perspective.
>
> I removed statements I was using that were damaging, for example, 'I'll get better at that and I have lots to learn,' thus removing the *subservient girl thing* with the 'I'm so grateful but don't know much' position.

I watched my manager's language and mirrored it with my own.

I found a format document for our meetings that my manager used. I started to own it and roll through it with the information he needed from me/my department.

I was amazed at how quickly things turned around once I started making these changes. One week later, at the end of a meeting, he said, "I'm so glad I've put you in this role Hannah, you are so commercial, switched on and focused on the business". To my delight, he shared this in front of other senior leaders. In the space of a week I had gone from a person who inspired doubt to a person who inspired confidence.

I went from being in tears each week after meetings and feeling like *I can't do this*, and aware that my manager thought I was green and incompetent, to the '*you are so commercial*' feedback. Our business relationship and my confidence have gone from strength to strength.

All it took was for Pollyanna to help me to identify my belief systems, language patterns and structure, and to get conscious about the whole conversation and the input needed to turn it around.

My confidence and delivery have risen ever since. One of the main things I recall Pollyanna saying, which shifted my approach was, 'Hannah, I don't want to hear that language again. Delete it, gone, no more. Only use 'I' messages when you own it'.

I'm still learning to break these language habits and I'm seeing real results by doing so. I now see how it undermined my position, making me appear less competent and viewed as a junior leader rather than the senior leader I am. It also portrayed me as insecure, which didn't help.

Pollyanna also said, 'He hired you for what you *do know*, not what you *don't know*. So what *do* you know that you can talk about?' I worked through the Three Phases of Awareness Model with Hannah to help her sort through her thoughts and communication of what she needed to take ownership of.

I designed the Three Phases of Awareness Model as a key underpinning framework I could use in my work with individuals, groups and teams.

The Three Phases of Awareness is a methodology that helps individuals to observe issues from the multiple perspectives of self, other, and climate. This broadens the lens and helps create a broader view of the situation; develop empathy for others; and heightens awareness of personal impact.

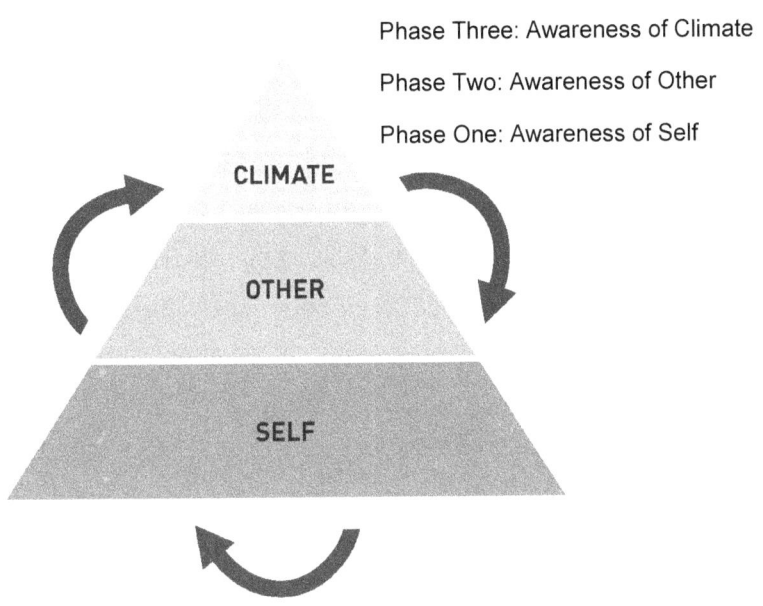

FIGURE 2: THREE PHASES OF AWARENESS MODEL

PHASE ONE: SELF-FOCUS

The focus here is on *self* and your personal opinions. This is where you view situations through the lens of *me*. How does this impact me? How do I feel? What's important to me?

Communication is from your perspective but with a focus on your desired outcomes and satisfaction of *self* and your personal agenda/outcomes.

When you are focusing on *self*, there is no attention to personal impact from this phase.

When I worked with Hannah, we looked at the situation from this lens first.

It's important to shine a light on what's important to you, what you want and how things are impacting you. The problem occurs when we stay fixed in this place and omit looking at how we are impacting others and the bigger picture. For example, have you ever been at a meeting, feeling nervous about what you were going to present. You stayed focused on this causing you to miss what was being said plus the nuances of what was unsaid. When you did speak up, the conversation had moved on and your point was either no longer relevant or had already been addressed.

PHASE TWO: FOCUS ON OTHER

Our attention is directed to the *other*, this is a hard laser-like focus.

Communication is from the perspectives of *other*. What is going on over there? A deep curiosity is peaked taking in the *others'* perspective.

There is an awareness of your impact on *others* from this phase.

Once Hannah had explored the situation from the viewpoint of *self*, we moved into *other*. I asked her to get deeply curious about what could be occurring for her manager by inviting her to be open to taking in his viewpoint and situation. What did he need from her that he wasn't getting?

What did she notice? How did this lens change the conversation?

What questions could she ask, from a perspective of *other*, to help her understand what was important to him and what his challenges were?

This shifted the focus away from herself and onto her manager. The questions and conversation that she had were very different from this place—she allowed space for his concerns and viewpoint, and provided an understanding of expectations. It also showed a level of empathy and understanding that was broader than that when she focused on herself.

PHASE THREE: FOCUS ON CLIMATE

Attention is widened to take in the complete picture: the environment, energy, what is said and not said is taken in. The culture of the environment, team or company is picked up here. You are aware of the mood or energy of the person to whom you are talking. You are aware of the atmosphere. This is the phase where we are in touch with our intuition.

The desired outcome here is **big picture awareness**.

There is greater awareness on attention to personal and group impact. To develop and consider the viewpoint required by the company. Here, Hannah focused on what the businesses needs were, connecting with the company's strategy and focus.

The next step in the process was to look at Hannah's communication style. How her communication approach was contributing to the situation and how could she reverse this. I noticed that Hannah overused 'I' messages, which resulted in her owning issues that did not belong to her.

In many communication programs, trainers refer to Dr Eric Berne's work with the ego states of Parent, Adult, Child. Dr Berne introduced *Transactional Analysis* in the 1950s stating that Parent, Adult and Child ego states exist in all of us and that these three modes determine how we treat ourselves as well as communicate with others.

The Parent

Physical: angry or impatient body language, finger pointing, patronising gestures.

Verbal: uses judgemental words (eg always, never, once and for all), critical words, patronising language, 'you' messages.

The Adult

Physical: fully engaged, assertive, listens actively

Verbal: 'I' messages – I think. I believe. I feel.

The Child

Physical: despair, tantrums, whining, giggling, sulking, rolling eyes.

Verbal: I want. Things never go right for me. I don't care.

Berne concluded that since communication is complementary, when we operate in parent mode the person we communicate with is forced to go into child mode and vice versa. Adult-to-Adult style communication is, therefore, the ideal style to create equal, effective and mutually beneficial relationships.

Used appropriately, this is still a sound communication strategy; however, 'I' messages are overused in both professional and personal environments by both men and women weakening communication, creating ownership of issues that don't belong to them and heightening stress levels. Women seem to be leading the charge with this one. Using 'I' causes you to take ownership, which can cause you to blame yourself for the issue rather than looking to the source of the problem. In addition, each time 'I' is used, others associate ownership to you. Try it. Think about a situation where ownership does not belong to you, then use 'I' statements aloud describing the situation and notice the impact it has on you. When doing this, even in a role-play, stress levels rise.

ONLY USE 'I' WHEN YOU OWN IT

Dr Phyllis Mindell (2001) talks about using 'I' in her book *How to Say it for Women*. If you haven't read her book, I recommend wholeheartedly to put it on your must-read list. It is a fabulous resource with practical examples and templates. She talks about how 'I' statements weaken language impact in several ways, and she shared the following five ways that this impacts *women*:

1. Opening up blame for issues that aren't yours.
2. Implying you're not sure of the facts.
3. Characterising inadequate leadership.
4. Harming women profoundly by making us appear immature and childlike.
5. Utilising weak childish 'I' statements 'fostering extensive psychobabble', which encourages 'touchy feely' emotional verbs rather than the action verbs that drive powerful language.

Dr Mindell shares the following example in her book.

Original: I have a problem with my secretary: he never gets to work on time.

Quick fix: My secretary has a problem: he never gets to work on time.

The second example puts the problem where it belongs—with the secretary not with the person discussing the situation.

Using a combination of awareness, language, ownership and wearing her *big girl pants* (stepping into her leadership and expertise), Hannah was able to reframe her situation, communicate from a place of strength and set firm boundaries around how she worked within the company. She talked about the importance of succession planning and team member development rather than what she couldn't do because she was 'just part-time on a 4-day week' and tired due to her pregnancy. This shift also gave her the tools and confidence to address her working hours and travel schedule to ensure that she wasn't placing undue risk and exhaustion on herself emotionally and physically.

She addressed the issues of *a lack of understanding* and *policy* from **Phase Three**: the impact to the company by having outdated diversity policies.

Communication, positioning and success

We also used Stephen Covey's circles of influence. I began by drawing three circles on a page.

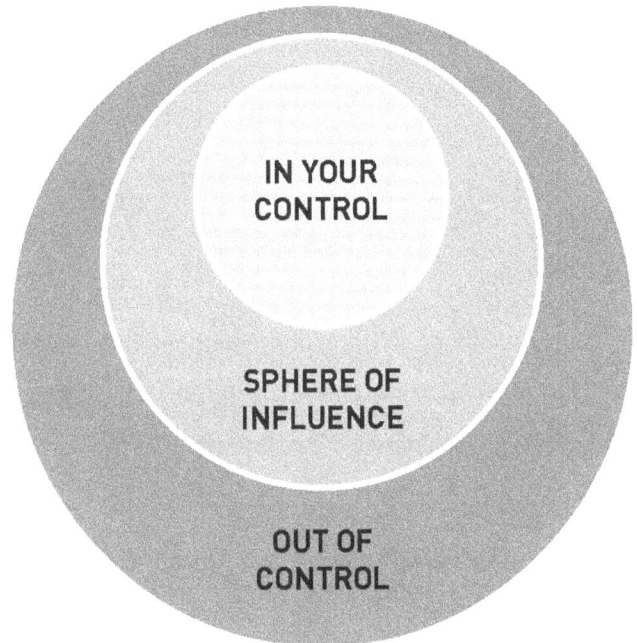

FIGURE 3: CIRCLES OF INFLUENCE

I asked Hannah what happens/how she feels when she focuses on something that is completely out of her control; when it is something that she can do nothing about. I asked her to do this from a place of *self*.

The following is a list of some of her replies:

— Loss of confidence

— Anxious

— Stressed

— Self-doubt creeps in

— Low self-esteem

- Get angry
- Start to blame
- Feel like a victim
- Feel powerless
- Exhausted
- Stuck
- I feel sick here.

Logically we know that focusing on something or a situation over which we have absolutely no control is futile and damaging to our health and wellbeing—physically, emotionally and mentally—yet, we still do this.

Welcome to the human condition; we are a hysterical species. What I love about Covey's model is that it provides a structure to lay it all out, which helps us examine the impact.

Next, I asked Hannah to share what happens/how she feels when she is able to influence a situation. I pointed out that influence did not necessarily mean that she always got her desired outcome but rather when she could influence the situation.

Her responses included:

- Feeling more in control
- More empowered
- Happier
- Less stuck (movement/momentum is created)
- More confident

- Accomplish more
- Self-esteem is higher
- More creative
- Get better results
- Higher levels of engagement.

Lastly, I asked her to share what happens/how she feels when she is able to control a situation. Her answers included:

- Feeling in control
- Empowered
- Confident
- Happy
- Energised
- Self-esteem is high
- Feel accomplished; I get things done.

Hannah noticed a lot of overlap between how she felt when she could influence and when she could control a situation.

For the final piece of this exercise, I asked Hannah to write down all the barriers she was facing in her current situation. When she had exhausted her list of barriers, I asked her to put them into the circles of influence. Once we established what was out of her control, she was able to stop consciously putting energy into and focusing upon these areas.

With the barriers that were in her sphere of influence and in her control, she was able to develop an action plan on how she would influence and control these.

Hannah resolved the following issues by using the tools provided in this section, enquiry through the coaching process and action. She used these processes in her current situation and many more afterwards. She was also able to avoid similar situations before they escalated.

She improved her brand/position in the company moving from a position where her abilities were doubted to a place of trusted advisor and strategist.

Using strong and powerful communication skills, she firmly established that she would be able to meet for half an hour at 9 pm before retiring for the evening; therefore, any items that required her input need to be discussed first.

She no longer absorbed issues that didn't belong to her, which positively impacted her self-confidence and reputation.

Her stress levels reduced and she was in a happier place.

Hannah delivered a healthy third addition to her family. She continues to work at a senior level enjoying her role and is mindful of ensuring she regularly puts on her big girl pants.

CASE STUDY: CASEY

Casey had risen to a senior level in her organisation. After a year's maternity leave, she rejoined her team and in her words: 'I felt like I had been hit by a bus. I would come home each night tired, emotional and feeling like a failure. I used to be that person who was dedicated, worked long hours and got things done'. Casey was running a script that fuelled self-doubt, criticism and judgement.

Casey was someone who still got things done, was still highly regarded and hadn't taken time to acknowledge that she was operating in a different landscape. Her priorities had changed when she added the dimension of motherhood into her world. She was still dedicated, still highly effective and was being incredibly hard on herself.

Operating from a space of self-doubt and giving in to feelings of *not doing enough* impacted Casey's confidence and self-esteem. It also affected how her team perceived her.

With a few simple changes Casey was able to step onto firmer ground. We looked at the language she was using and made some changes.

Old	New
I'm just part-time	My hours are ...
Sorry, I'm late	I noticed you scheduled the meeting at 9 am, I can attend from 9.30 am. Let's reschedule future meetings so the whole team can attend.
I have to take a lesser role now that I am part-time.	I want to explore and work towards my next role.
I'm not contactable after 3 pm	The best times to connect with me are ...

Casey realised that she had developed a perception that she was always late—especially problematic for the senior leadership meeting that was scheduled at 9 am each Monday morning. She wasn't late. Her contracted hours were 9.30 am – 4 pm. With agreement from her organisation, she worked part-time over 5 days to work within her childcare arrangements.

Her fellow team members were unaware of this and would feel resentment toward Casey's late arrival. A team member shared, 'I don't have children to sympathise but it's not an excuse to be late for every team meeting'. Once that team member realised that Casey wasn't late and that she wasn't being disrespectful nor was she expecting special consideration, their relationship and dynamic changed.

Casey approached her manager to talk with the team to reposition the expectations of what she was able to achieve—given the hours she worked—not just for herself but for all team members who were working flexible hours.

All future meetings that required Casey to attend were scheduled within her working hours and Casey reframed how she communicated this. This had an impact not only on the team, by providing an opportunity to discuss the unconscious bias that was prevalent, but to also help Casey realign with her decisions, set boundaries and communicate from a more assertive and positive place.

Think about how you communicate and where some simple changes would provide more a positive and stronger impact.

AFTERWORD

WHAT IS SUCCESS?

SUCCESS IS WHAT IT MEANS TO YOU.

For me success is how I feel about who I am, my place in the world, the contribution I make and the people in my life. It's about aligning the things I do in my life to the bigger picture of who I am being and becoming.

Thank you for reading my book. It's my sincerest hope that these words and stories have provoked reflection and insight for you and have helped you on your journey.

I ask that you continue this reflection and ignite discussion with other women about success and what it means to them, while also sharing what it means to you.

Engage this conversation across generations to learn more about the women in your life.

GLOSSARY

New biology

The branch of biology that deals with the nature of biological phenomena at the molecular level through the study of DNA and RNA, proteins, and other macromolecules involved in genetic information and cell function, characteristically making use of advanced tools and techniques of separation, manipulation, imaging and analysis. (Source: Dictionary.com)

Neuroscience

Any or all of the sciences such as neurochemistry and experimental psychology, which deal with the structure or function of the nervous system or brain. (Source: Dictionary.com)

SUPPORT GROUPS LIST

Be kind to yourself. If something emerges for you when performing the exercises in this book, please seek professional support. Below is a list of Australian organisations; please refer to an organisation local to you. It would also be worth asking your company if they provide an Employee Assist Program.

www.beyondblue.org.au

www.depression.com.au

www.blackdoginstitute.org.au

www.headspace.org.au

www.depressionet.com.au

www.counsellingaustralia.com.au

www.australiacounselling.com.au

www.salvoscounselling.salvos.org.au

CONTRIBUTORS AND SPECIAL MENTIONS

Amanda Simoes, I thank you every day. Befriending you dramatically changed my health and wellbeing.

Amanda had changed her life. She had had a glamourous career and a loving partner and lost it all through alcoholism. Today, Amanda is changing the lives of others through her talks on alcoholism, alcohol abuse, misuse and binge drinking. Speaking in schools, organisations and public forums. Her website is www.alcohol-speaker.co.uk. Amanda has been sober for 25 years. She remains a dear friend.

Tracy Fitzpatrick, thank you for sharing your knowledge and expertise and for helping me to *Change the Sentence*.

Tracy Fitzpatrick is a qualified, senior executive coach and mentor with extensive business and corporate experience. Tracy's 20 years' experience in international sales management has led her to solely now focus on people who want or need to sell: themselves, products or services. Her success stems from the delivery of her 'sales behaviour' workshops, coaching and e-learning modules.

Tracy Fitzpatrick

Tracy.fitzpatrick2@gmail.com

The Women, Work & Success report was designed, conducted and distributed by Pollyanna Lenkic, and analysed and prepared by **Mark Bahnisch**, BA *Qld* BComm (Hons) (First Class) *Griff,* graddipBus (distinction) *QUT.*

Rick Tamlyn remains an inspiration to me. He inspires others to *play their bigger game*. You can visit Rick's website www.ricktamlyn.com for information on keynotes, interactive training, workshops and coaching.

WORKS CITED

Anon., 2013. *High-achievers suffering from 'impostor syndrome'.* [Online]
Available at: http://www.news.com.au/finance/highachievers-suffering-from-imposter-syndrome/story-e6frfm1i-1226779707766

Anon., 2015. *VIA Survey of Character Strenghths.* s.l.:VIA Institute on Character.

Anon., n.d. [Online]
Availabe at: www.coachinc.com

Anon., n.d. [Online]
Available at: www.brucelipton.com

Anon., n.d. *Coaches Training Institute.* [Online]
Available at: www.thecoaches.com

Anon., n.d. *Coaches Training Institute.* [Online]
Available at: www.thecoaches.com/leadership

Ballinger, L., n.d. *How clothes can boost mood.* [Online]
Available at:
http://www.bodyandsoul.com.au/weight+loss/body+confidence/how+clothes+can+boost+mood,15461

Ban Breathnach, S., 2012. *Peace and plenty: Finding your path to financial serenity.* s.l.:Grand Central Publishing.

Beaudoin, M.-N., 1998. *Working with groups to enhance relationships.* s.l.:Whole Person Associates. Inc.

Bennetts, L., 2007. *The Feminine Mistake: Are we giving up too much?.* s.l.:Voice.

Berne, E., 2015. *Transactional Analysis.* [Online]
Available at: http://www.ericberne.com/transactional-analysis/

Brown, B., 2010. *The gifts of imperfection: Let go of who you think you're supposed to be and embrace who you are.* s.l.:Hazelden.

Brown, B., 2010. *The power of vulnerability.* s.l.:TEDx.

Carroll, L., 1920. *Alice in Wondeland.* s.l.:Macmillan.

Carson, R. D., 2003. *Taming your Gremlin: A surprisingly simple method for getting out of your own way.* New York: William Morrow & Company.

Chopra, D., 2014. *Deepak Chopra's 7-step exercise to release emotional turbulence.* [Online]
Available at: http://life.gaiam.com/article/deepak-chopras-7-step-exercise-release-emotional-turbulence

Clance, P. R., 2013. [Online]
Available at: http://www.paulineroseclance.com/impostor_phenomenon.html

Clance, P. R. & Imes, S., 1978. *The Impostor Syndrome in High Achieving Women: Dymanics and Therapeutic intervention,* s.l.: Georgie State Unversity.

Coles, A., 2003. *Alice Coles of Bayview : Model Resident transformed poor village into modern community* [Interview] (26 November 2003).

Covey, S. R., 1989. *The 7 Habits of Highly Effective People.* New York: Simon & Schuster.

Donald, B., 2013. Babies whose efforts are priased become more motivated kids, say Stanford researchers. *Stanford News,* 12 February.

Dweck, C. S., 2007. *Mindset: The New Psychology of Success.* s.l.:Ballantine Books.

Gilbert, E., 2006. *Eat, Pray, Love.* s.l.:Riverhead Books.

Gilbert, E., 2009. *Your elusive creative genius.* s.l.:TEDx.

Gladwell, M., 2011. *Outliers: The story of success.* s.l.:Back Bay Books.

Halligan, P., 2005. Where belief is born. *The Guardian,* 30 June.

Hawking, S., 1998. *A brief history of time.* s.l.:Bantam.

Imes, S., 2015. [Online]
Available at: http://www.suzanneimes.com/

Kay, K. & Shipman, C., 2014. *The Confidence Gap.* [Online]
Available at: http://www.theatlantic.com/features/archive/2014/04/the-confidence-gap/359815/

Kay, K. & Shipman, C., 2015. [Online]
Available at: http://theconfidencecode.com/

Kormas, S., 2006. *The Centre for Management Creativity.* [Online]
Available at: http://www.get2cmc.com.au/aboutus.htm
[Accessed 15 May 2015].

Lipton, B. H., 2007. *The Biology of Belief: Unleashing the Power of Consciousness, Matter & Miracles.* s.l.:Hay House.

M.D, D. E. B., 1964. *Games People Play.* 1st ed. s.l.:Penguin.

Mainiero, L. A. & Sullivan, S. E., 2005. *Kaleidoscope Careers: An alternative explanation for the 'opt-out' revolution,* s.l.: Academy of Management Executive.

McLeod, S. A., 2007. *Maslow's Heirarchy of Needs.* [Online]
Available at: www.simplypsychology.org/maslow

Mindell, P., 2001. How to Say It For Women: Communicating with Confidence and Power Using the Language of Success. In: s.l.:Prentice Hall Press, p. 27.

Mindell, P., 2001. *How to say it women: communicating with confidence and power using the launguage of success.* s.l.:Prentice Hall Press.

O'Callaghan, J., 2014. You are what you dress: clothing has a significant effect on self-esteem and confidence, claims expert. *Daily Mail Australia*, 31 May.

OFM, R. R., n.d. *Discharging your loyal soldier.* [Sound Recording].

Palmer, B., n.d. [Online]
Available at: www.thatpeoplething.com

Pine, K. J., 2014. *Mind what you wear: the psychology of fashion,* s.l.: s.n.

Plotkin, B., 2003. *Soulcraft: Crossing into the Mysteries of Nature and Psyche*. s.l.:New World Library.

Sandberg, S., 2013. *Lean In: Women, work and the will to lead*. s.l.:Knopf.

Tamlyn, R., 2013. *Play your bigger game: 9 minutes to learn, a lifetime to live*. s.l.:Hay House.

Weir, K., 2013. *Feel like a fraud?*. [Online]
Available at: http://www.apa.org/gradpsych/2013/11/fraud.aspx

Williamson, M., 1996. *A return to love: reflections on the principles of "a course in miracles"*. s.l.:HarperOne.

Young, V., 2011. *The secret thoughts of successful women: why capable people suffer from the impostor syndrome and how to thrive in spite of it*. s.l.:Crown Business.

MORE ABOUT THE AUTHOR

'For me, success is how I feel about who I am; my place in the world; the contribution I make; and the people in my life. It is about aligning the things I do in my life to the bigger picture of who I am being and becoming.'

Pollyanna Lenkic is passionate about bringing the discussion and exploration of what success means to women, how they see themselves through the lens of success and the impact this has on their lives and the lives of others, at home, at work and globally.

She has spent the past 15 years studying, researching and exploring women and their relationship to success. She believes strongly that the issue of women and success is a business and global issue, not a women's issue. Understanding how women see and define themselves through the lens of success is an important discovery for both women and men. This discovery helps to understand how to promote success and to maximise potential to the benefit of the individual, the organisation and the world.

Pollyanna is interviewed regularly by magazines and regional newspapers as a subject expert on women and success. In 2006, Pollyanna designed, conducted then launched the results of *Women, Work & Success;* a first of its kind report in Australia about how women perceive success.

Pollyanna is the founder of the Women & Success series: a suite of mentoring and leadership programs run within organisations and for entrepreneurial groups. She regularly hosts Gender Balance Forums gathering industry leaders and providing the opportunity for executives (from these organisations) to share experiences and strategies in implementing gender balance in their organisation.

In addition to her work in this area, Pollyanna's other passion is helping organisations build sustainable high-performing teams. She writes, as an expert on teams, for SmartCompany, an online magazine that provides business news, advice and information for Australian SMEs.

Prior to her work as a coach and mentor, Pollyanna co-founded a specialist IT recruitment consultancy in London in 1990. In November 2000, she sold her 50% shareholding having taken the company from a sole-employee entity to a staff of 18 and a contract workforce of 100+ consultants with an annual turnover in excess of £11m.

Pollyanna is committed to community projects and networking groups that help people move forward both personally and professionally. She has mentored in the Marketing Women's mentoring program in Melbourne and was involved in two mentoring projects in London: the Du Paul Trust, a UK- based charity, which works with people who are homeless, and Women in Banking and Finance. For two years she served as an advisor to the board of The 100, a cross generational women's networking group. She served on the leadership team of the ICFV (International Coach Federation Victorian) from 2006–2009 as Secretary and as Co-President of the ICF Victorian Chapter.

To find out more about Pollyanna Lenkic, including her *Women, Work & Success* survey, and her mentoring and coaching programs, visit pollyannalenkic.com or email her at pollyanna@pollyannalenkic.com.

WOMEN TALK ABOUT SUCCESS

(RESPONSES FROM WOMEN WHO PARTICIPATED IN THE
WOMEN, WORK AND SUCCESS SURVEY 2006)

'Success is how I have been able to develop wisdom by learning more and more about my delusions and illusions, and connecting to what is sustainable compared to what is not sustainable.'

'Success is the satisfaction I get when I see the growth and development in those I have assisted. Success is being happy in my employment, having a balanced home and work life, and a happy family.'

'[Success is] a sense of passion to achieve, belief in [my] own abilities, and life-long learning. (You will never know it all).'

'My view of success for me is less about position and more about feeling comfortable in my own skin'

'Through the team spirit and often family philosophy that I had created within this group of people, I feel that I have achieved success'

'My rating of success is dependent on how I have been able to help others and have been able to make some small difference to those who come in contact with my company'

'Success is also about how I have been able to develop wisdom by learning more and more about my delusions and illusions, and connecting to what is sustainable compared to what is not sustainable'

'Success is being happy in my employment, having a balanced home and work life and being a happy family'

'Feeling fulfilment and balance with life and with work. Living true to my values'

www.ingramcontent.com/pod-product-compliance
Lightning Source LLC
Chambersburg PA
CBHW071416160426
43195CB00013B/1707